Leadership transcends titles; it's a dynamic practice shaping organisations and societies. This book, rooted in decades of governmental experience, explores the essence of leadership, emphasising inspiration, collaboration, and a vision for the greater good. It advocates balancing confidence with empathy and integrity, highlighting the importance of innovation and inclusivity in fostering lasting impact and collective well-being.

Ahmaddin Abdul Rahman
Minister for Home Affairs, Brunei

In a world that has become so divided and lacks leadership, this book couldn't come at a better time. A very easy read and practical handbook to become a leader who serves the people with a purpose and conviction, from an inspiring and humble civil servant.

Chea Serey
Governor of the National Bank of Cambodia

Yong Soon's book offers a robust, practical framework for mastering the art of leadership. He compellingly argues that while personality can influence leadership style, true leaders are made through dedication and learning. This book is a valuable resource for anyone aiming to become a more effective and empathetic leader committed to creating lasting impact.

Cheng Wai Keung
Deputy Chairman of Temasek Holdings
Chairman of Wing Tai Holdings
Chairman of SingHealth

The need for wise and effective leadership is universal. In his clear and concise way, Tan Yong Soon distils advice from the experts – from Aristotle to the *Harvard Business Review* – together with diverse experiences from successful Asian leaders. The result is a valuable 'how-to' guide for our next generation's leaders.

Dame DeAnne Julius
Chairman of Chatham House (Royal Institute of International Affairs) (2003-2012)
Chair of the Council at University College London (2014-2019)

The Singapore of today is a miracle. The miracle would not have happened if we didn't have great leaders. This is why Yong Soon's book on leadership is so important.

Tommy Koh
Ambassador-at-Large, Ministry of Foreign Affairs, Singapore

Yong Soon offers many useful lessons for public servants at all levels. They are not just ideas and principles; they work! Up-and-coming leaders in the private sector and the non-profits can also benefit much if they wish to lead better and to exercise more influence for good.

Lim Siong Guan
Head, Civil Service, Singapore (1999-2005)
Group President of GIC, Singapore's sovereign wealth fund (2007-2016)

Tan Yong Soon has created an interesting book on leadership that should galvanise readers into focusing on the essentials of that elusive art.

J.Y. Pillay
Chairman of the Council of Presidential Advisers, Singapore (2005-2018)
First Chairman of Singapore Airlines (1972-1996)

Yong Soon's book, based on his lectures as Professor of Practice in the Lee Kuan Yew School of Public Policy, is more than a textbook on public service leadership. He roams far and wide, drawing on his extensive research on the concept of leadership and his personal experience as a senior public service leader. He includes short essays and interview transcripts by iconic Singapore public service leaders such as Lim Siong Guan and J.Y. Pillay and several other ASEAN personalities. Our public servants, as well as non-Singaporeans, will benefit from Yong Soon's clear and useful elucidation of leadership.

Eddie Teo
Chairman of Council of Presidential Advisers, Singapore (2019-)
Chairman of Public Service Commission, Singapore (2008-2018)

PUBLIC SERVICE
LEADERSHIP

Lead Better to Achieve Success and Happiness

PUBLIC SERVICE LEADERSHIP

◆

Lead Better to Achieve Success and Happiness

Tan Yong Soon

Professor of Practice, Lee Kuan Yew School of Public Policy,
National University of Singapore

Former Permanent Secretary in the Singapore Civil Service

World Scientific

NEW JERSEY · LONDON · SINGAPORE · BEIJING · SHANGHAI · HONG KONG · TAIPEI · CHENNAI

Published by

World Scientific Publishing Co. Pte. Ltd.

5 Toh Tuck Link, Singapore 596224

USA office: 27 Warren Street, Suite 401-402, Hackensack, NJ 07601

UK office: 57 Shelton Street, Covent Garden, London WC2H 9HE

National Library Board, Singapore Cataloguing in Publication Data
Name(s): Tan, Yong Soon.
Title: Public service leadership : lead better to achieve success and happiness / Tan Yong Soon.
Description: Singapore : World Scientific Publishing Co. Pte. Ltd., [2024]
Identifier(s): ISBN 978-981-12-9817-2 (hardback) | 978-981-98-0022-3 (paperback) |
    978-981-12-9818-9 (ebook for institutions) | 978-981-12-9819-6 (ebook for individuals)
Subject(s): LCSH: Public administration--Singapore. | Leadership--Singapore.
Classification: DDC 352.2305957--dc23

British Library Cataloguing-in-Publication Data
A catalogue record for this book is available from the British Library.

For any available supplementary material, please visit
https://www.worldscientific.com/worldscibooks/10.1142/13983#t=suppl

Desk Editor: Jiang Yulin
Design and layout: Loo Chuan Ming

In memory of my parents

About the Book

What is the role of a leader? Why do you want to be a leader? Can anyone be a leader? *Public Service Leadership* will help you answer these questions and more.

Drawing on the rich public service leadership experience of the author, this book introduces the five practices of good leadership (Clarity, Courage, Communications, Caring-ness and Culture); demonstrates how you can be a leader by managing yourself, your boss and luck; and explores the fulfilment of life goals such as success, happiness and friendship.

While the book is about public service leadership, the lessons and stories can also be applied to leaders in the private and non-profit sectors. Even those holding middle or junior positions of organisations can discover how to be better leaders.

Contents

About the Author

Tan Yong Soon started his career in the Singapore Armed Forces (SAF) when he won an SAF Overseas Scholarship in 1974 to study at Cambridge University, UK. Upon graduation in 1977, he served in various staff and command appointments, mostly staff appointments in planning, intelligence and policy areas. He topped his Command and Staff Course in 1982, and graduated with a Masters in Public Administration from Harvard University Kennedy School of Government in 1988 and was selected to receive one of the first four Josephine and Raymond Vernon prizes for academic distinction in the Edward S. Mason Program. He was promoted to Brigadier General in 1993 and was awarded the Public Administration Medal (Gold) (Military) in 1994. The award citation stated that "BG Tan Yong Soon promoted and effectively managed Singapore's defence relations. He directed a more effective presentation of SAF's image and defence policies, and developed a landmark framework for the formulation of long-term strategies and policies".

Tan Yong Soon left the SAF to join the Administrative Service in 1995. He has held positions of Deputy Secretary (Policy) in the Ministry of Defence, Principal Private Secretary to the Prime Minister, Deputy Secretary (Revenue) and Deputy Secretary (Policy) in the Ministry of Finance, Chief Executive Officer of the Urban Redevelopment Authority, Permanent Secretary (Perm Sec) of the Ministry of Environment and

Water Resources (MEWR) and Perm Sec in the National Climate Change Secretariat (NCCS) in the Prime Minister's Office.

As Perm Sec of MEWR, he played an important role in growing Singapore's water and environment industry, enhancing Singapore's living environment and raising Singapore's international profile in the environmental arena. He oversaw many major programmes, such as the opening of Singapore's first desalination plant, the development of NEWater plants, the completion of Marina Barrage and the inauguration of the annual Singapore International Water Week. He helped to develop a clean and healthy environment for all Singaporeans to enjoy.

As the first Perm Sec of NCCS, he laid strong foundations, developed strategy and built new capabilities to understand and address the challenges posed by climate change.

Tan Yong Soon retired from the Civil Service in late 2012 and joined the Lee Kuan Yew School of Public Policy, first as an Adjunct Professor and later as Professor of Practice where he teaches public service and leadership. He is the founding director of the Lee Kuan Yew Senior Fellowship in Public Service programme which was started in 2019.

Preface

Mr Lee Kuan Yew on his 80th birthday in 2003 agreed to have the public policy school in the National University of Singapore named after him. He wanted the school to be the venue for scholars, officials and students from the world over to gather, conduct research and exchange ideas on how societies are best governed in a globalising world. Mr Lee Kuan Yew had devoted his life to making Singapore a success. But he was also thinking beyond Singapore, sharing Singapore's brand of governance, contributing to the transformation of the region and improving the lives of its people. With his support, the school was able to raise huge donations and attracted promising students from all over Asia and beyond.

In 2012, as my retirement from the public service drew near, I was invited by my friend and former Civil Service colleague, Kishore Mahbubani, Dean of the Lee Kuan Yew School of Public Policy (LKYSPP), to join the faculty as an adjunct professor.

I have had a public service career of more than 35 years, about half of which was spent in the military and the other half in the Civil Service. I have been very fortunate in my career – given good training opportunities, exposed to challenging job experiences, learning from good bosses and colleagues. I wanted to share my knowledge and public service experience with younger public servants. LKYSPP is ideal.

LKYSPP is a postgraduate school with a diverse student population. Only 20 percent of its students are from Singapore. The students are a mix of mid-career officers (mostly in public service, some in non-profits and a few in the private sector), as well as fresh graduates and those with only a few years of working experience.

My public service career credentials helped, but it is not easy to be a teacher. Much preparation is needed. The adjunct position is a good way to ease into academia. It offers no pay and requires no minimum teaching workload, but would pay a stipend for each course module I choose to teach. Meanwhile, I learned more about the university and the school, met faculty members and staff, and attended events and talks held at the school.

When I was ready, I chose to teach leadership rather than specific subjects such as fiscal policy, urban management and environmental sustainability which I had work experience in because I believe leadership is key. At all levels, we need leaders. Leaders who can articulate a clear and compelling vision. Leaders who can inspire and mobilise their people to give their best to achieve the vision. Leaders who have the moral courage to do what is right even when it may not be popular. Leaders who care about the people they lead and serve.

I dug into my years of public service experience and reading, trying to recollect what I wish I knew when I was in my 30s. I designed the course to enable students to better understand the concepts and practice of leadership and develop a better knowledge of public service. The course also aims to help the student discover for himself how to be a better leader at whichever level or position he holds.

I called my module Public Service Leadership because my background and experience is in public service. There are some differences between public and private sector leadership. Leadership in public service combines the political and administrative, and requires a good understanding of citizens, complexity and communications.

But the focus on leadership is the same, whether in the public service or private sector. Both public service and private sector leaders have to implement necessary actions to achieve desired results. I began teaching the module in Academic Year 2015/6.

Whether the students are in the public service or non-profit/private sector, whether they aspire to be a leader or otherwise, my hope is for them to learn from my course on how to do their job better, reach their potential and find purpose.

The students learned not just from me, but also from one another. The best learning is from one's peers. They also benefitted from experienced guest speakers whom I invited to share with the class. At the same time, I learned from the students. The students were a real joy to teach. As Claudia Goldin, Harvard Professor of Economics, said at the press conference after winning the 2023 Nobel Prize (for tracking American women's labour participation over centuries, and the evolution of the wage gap): "I am standing here because I have students. My students are my muses. My students are the individuals I depend upon to listen to my ideas and to react to them." I too depend on my students. With their feedback, my course evolved and improved.

In 2018, I accepted the position of Professor of Practice with the school. I also took on the responsibility of creating a new programme, the Lee Kuan Yew Senior Fellowship in Public Service. It was a privilege to help shape senior leaders from Asia and beyond, to expand their vision and ambitions, and to challenge them to deliver better outcomes for the benefit of their people, communities and societies.

I decided to write this book based on my Public Service Leadership module at LKYSPP. The book contains leadership lessons on how to become a better public service leader, which I hope readers will find useful. It includes a few short essays penned by experienced practitioners and excerpts of an interview with Mr J.Y. Pillay to give a broader understanding of leadership.

It is important for each and every one of us to be a leader!

Tan Yong Soon
Professor of Practice
Lee Kuan Yew School of Public Policy
National University of Singapore
August 2024

Acknowledgements

I wish to thank my parents, teachers and bosses who have taught me leadership.

My parents came to Singapore from Chao'an, Chaozhou, China. They had only a few years of formal education and were poor. But they raised eight children and taught me the values of integrity, responsibility, benevolence and gratitude, and the importance of character.

Many teachers not only imparted knowledge but showed they cared. Mr Hector Chee, my Secondary 3/4 maths teacher, was resourceful and innovative in introducing modern maths to our school and later, Singapore. I enjoyed maths and did well under his teaching. I also learned how to take calculated risks. Mr Lim Kim Woon, principal of National Junior College, was inspirational and energetic, and taught us to be good citizens.

I have learned from so many bosses throughout my career but it is not possible to name them all. As a young graduate, I was posted to 7th Battalion, Singapore Infantry Regiment. My commanding officer was Major Tham. He led by example and exacted high standards from his men and officers. I learned how to lead and command the respect of soldiers.

I had the good fortune of working closely with Mr Lim Siong Guan for many years. I learned much from his thinking and actions. He was an exemplary leader, a superb teacher and a great developer of people.

I was also privileged to work directly under Mr Goh Chok Tong: as his Military Personal Secretary when he first became the Minister for Defence, and later as the Principal Private Secretary to the Prime Minister. Not only was I exposed to policymaking at a very high level, I learned much from Mr Goh: vision, calmness, genuine concern for people, willingness to listen, the ability to inspire, the courage to make tough decisions, among other things.

I have benefitted from many colleagues throughout my career: in the SAF and Mindef, MOF, PMO, URA, ENV, PUB, NEA and NCCS, and those with whom I have worked on projects, such as the first national scenario planning project team in 1992-1993 and the setting up of Power 98 radio station.

I am thankful for the opportunity to teach at the Lee Kuan Yew School after my retirement from the Civil Service, first as Adjunct Professor and then as Professor of Practice.

I thank my students in the Public Service Leadership course, which I have conducted every year since AY2015, for their participation and enthusiasm. Their feedback on my teaching has been valuable. They also help update me on public service practices in Singapore and elsewhere. I thank particularly Bao Yilun, an MPA student in my AY 2023 class, for agreeing to include her essay in this book.

I thank my guest lecturers who came to share their leadership experiences with my students: Mr J.Y. Pillay, Khoo Boon Hui (former Commissioner of Police and Interpol President), Cheng Hsing Yao (former URA colleague who transited successfully from public service to the private sector and is now CEO of a major real estate group) and Tan Lai Yong (medical doctor who did extensive voluntary work in poverty alleviation and community development in China).

I also thank participants of the LKY Senior Fellowship in Public Service programme which I started in 2019. The senior fellows come from all over the world and are exceptional. I have learned much from them, and from the distinguished speakers and professors who share their knowledge and experience during the programme.

I am especially grateful to Chua Soon Guan, Lee Peck Ping, Dayna Lim, Aaron Loh, Winnie Tan, Tan Yanqiang, Mark Wong and Yeo Teck Yong for reviewing an early draft of this book; and Hong Hai, Ling Sing Lin and Tan Yanqiang for reading the first proofs. Their invaluable feedback and comments helped improve the book immeasurably.

I am most appreciative of the essays from Ahmaddin Abdul Rahman, Cham Tao Soon, Chua Chin Kiat, Hong Hai, Pum Huot, Tommy Koh, Kelvin Lester K. Lee, Lim Siong Guan, Yanuar Nugroho, Tan Eng Chye and the use of J.Y. Pillay's interview excerpts. They are established leaders in their chosen career. The inclusion of their take on leadership has made the book richer.

I thank Chua Hong Koon, Publishing Director of World Scientific Publishing (WSP), for his persuasion and persistence in getting me to finally write the book; Triena Ong, book editor, for her tight editing and excellent suggestions, which have made this book more readable; and Jiang Yulin, Senior Editor of WSP, for his very efficient management of the book completion.

I am honoured to have the book endorsed by Ahmaddin Abdul Rahman, Chea Serey, Cheng Wai Keung, DeAnne Julius, Tommy Koh, Lim Siong Guan, J.Y. Pillay, and Eddie Teo.

Most of all, I would like to thank my wife and children for their love and support, without which this project could not have been undertaken.

PART 1

WHAT IS LEADERSHIP?

art 1 of this book comprises four chapters. Chapter 1 describes what leaders do, namely the V.I.P. functions of Visioning, Implementation and People engagement and development. Leaders must provide direction, deliver outcomes and care deeply for their people.

Chapter 2 explains the difference between managing and leading, and why both are important. We must both lead and manage.

Chapter 3 prods readers to ask themselves why they want to lead. To lead is to serve; it is not an entitlement. A leader must be able to deliver a better outcome for his people. Public service leaders serve two groups of people: the first group comprises the officers working within the organisation, and the second group comprises people served by the organisation and members of the public. We should deliver a better outcome for both groups, with priority given to members of the public and the people served by the organisation.

Chapter 4 reminds readers that leadership is not the preserve of those at the top. Everyone at every level can and must lead. We must all learn to be leaders.

Finally, while personality does matter, leaders are made and not born. We can all learn to be leaders. We must all be better leaders.

Part 1 ends with an essay "Short Thoughts on Leadership" by Mr Lim Siong Guan. He reminds us that the unending challenge of leadership is to Think People, Think Future and Think Excellence. Lim Siong Guan had been a Permanent Secretary in a number of ministries, Head of the Civil Service, Chairman of the Economic Development Board and Group President of the Government of Singapore Investment Corporation. He is an excellent public service leader who has made big improvements to the Singapore Public Service. I have worked with Siong Guan for many years and learned much from him. I may have internalised his teaching because I use the V.I.P. model to describe a leader. V for Visioning is akin to Think Future. I for Implementation is akin to Think Excellence. P for People engagement and development is akin to Think People.

CHAPTER 1

What Does a Leader Do?

A leader must be able to deliver a better outcome for his people. To lead is to serve, to instil hope and to identify the pathways to a better future for our people. The leader's job is to achieve results, <u>with</u> people and <u>through</u> people – results which the people could not have achieved by themselves, without the leader.

The leader does this through **the V.I.P. functions**:

- <u>V</u>isioning
- effective <u>I</u>mplementation
- engaging and developing the <u>P</u>eople working with him.

Visioning

A leader is only a leader if he has followers. Why do people follow a leader? If we are in an organisation, we have to follow the person whom we report to in the hierarchy. But the best people don't just follow any person whom they report to. It's not whom they follow; it's what they follow. They follow the leader's cause or vision. The leader is but an embodiment of that purpose. You can't be a leader whom people want to follow if you are without vision.

The vision must be compelling. Why? People want progress and aspire to a better future. They will follow a leader whom they believe will lead them towards progress and fulfil their hopes and dreams.

Antoine de Saint-Exupery, author of *The Little Prince*, wrote in his book *Citadelle* (Chicago University Press, 1984): "If you want to build a ship, don't drum up people to collect wood and don't assign them tasks and work, but rather teach them to long for the endless immensity of the sea." Of course, shipwrights need to have extensive knowledge about construction, and to know engineering and maths. And seamen must possess seafaring skills such as knot-tying, navigation and communications skills. The ability to work with others is also important because it takes a team to build a ship and sail a ship. But it is the excitement and the immense possibilities of the sea that motivate and inspire them.

The vision must motivate. A month after Singapore was forced to leave Malaysia, when Singaporeans were feeling insecure about the future, then Prime Minister Lee Kuan Yew painted a bright future for Singapore.

In a speech at the Sree Narayana Mission on 12 September 1965, he told Singaporeans:

"Over 100 years ago, this was a mud-flat, swamp. Today, this is a modern city. Ten years from now, this will be a metropolis. Never fear."

From mud-flat to metropolis. The vision resonated with Singaporeans. They rallied behind Lee Kuan Yew, and the rest is history.

A good vision must have content, credibility and commitment. The vision painted in the September 1965 speech had content because

Lee Kuan Yew was addressing what Singaporeans wanted and needed at that point of their history. He gave hope and reassurance to the people.

The vision had credibility because Lee Kuan Yew had demonstrated grit and gumption, the track record, expertise and gravitas to overcome the odds. People trusted that he would deliver.

And the vision also requires commitment. People must own the vision and be willing to work for it. Lee Kuan Yew called on Singaporeans to remember that every Singaporean had contributed to the nation's growth in the past: "You helped build it; your fathers, your grandfathers helped build this. There was no naval base here, and it is not the British who built it. It was your labour, your father's labour which built that. My (great) grandfather came here and built." Singaporeans understood they had a stake and wanted to work towards achieving the vision.

This commitment must be from everyone. For Lee Kuan Yew, a divided society would not do. He made the speech at the Sree Narayana Mission in Sembawang to emphasise the importance of tolerance, multilingualism and multiracialism; that Singapore was a multireligious, multicultural society. He began the speech stating that he was presenting scholarships worth $100/- each to 10 students, not only to Indian students. The money probably came from Indian donors because they were members of the Mission, but the scholarships were also being given to Malays and Chinese too. It is such gestures that make for harmony and understanding. He assured the minority races and promised a multiracial society. He called for Singaporeans to embrace other Singaporeans of different races: "Here we make the model multi-racial society. This is not a country that belongs to any single community: it belongs to all of us." He signalled his commitment by promising that "there will be a Constitution which we will get re-drawn in which minority rights … will be entrenched and enforceable."

Implementation

A compelling vision and good policy mean nothing if the implementation is poor. As Thomas Edison said, "Vision without execution is hallucination."

Leaders must be effective at implementation to produce positive, tangible and measurable results.

Problems of implementation include issues of how to influence behaviour, overcome resistance, lead change, align the organisation, form functional teams, provide resources, transform successfully and get people to achieve results which they could not otherwise do by themselves.

Whether it is seeking information/approval or making a decision, defining the right problem and asking the right questions is key: Who, where, how and what do we ask? Who and what do we trust? What do we know and, just as importantly, what do we not know? What are our biases? How do we decide? What are the consequences?

Decisions must be based on evidence. We need to listen to the experts but be cognisant of their limitations. Experts could also be blindsided and lured into groupthink. In the end, experts advise but leaders decide.

In order to obtain feedback, leaders must spend time with their followers, customers, citizens and stakeholders to understand their needs and how they think. Good ideas can surface from both top-down and ground-up.

Seeking opinions and information also enables leaders to avoid echo chambers that reinforce what they think is true. Isolation and surrounding himself with yes-men will leave the leader out of touch and out of tune.

In the end, leaders must lead. It is the leader's job. It is not practical, and sometimes even foolhardy, to design policy, programmes or products by focus groups. As Henry Ford, the founder of Ford Motor Company which produced the mass-assembled Model T that helped put the world on wheels, famously said, "If I had asked what people wanted, they would have said faster horses." Or in the words of Akio Morita, Sony Chairman, who invented the Walkman, the world's first portable music player that was introduced in 1979, "The public does not know what is possible. We do."

Public service leaders must be able to lead, make unpopular decisions and yet win popular support. As Lee Kuan Yew told Members of Parliament on 23 February 1977, "Popular government does not mean that you do popular things all the time ... Popular, representative government means that within each five-year period, your policies have demonstrably worked and won popular support. That is what it means. And if we flinch from the unpopular, we are in deep trouble."

The leader must understand the relationship between authority, responsibility and accountability. Authority is power: the power and ability to control and direct. The leader may be delegated such power or he may have won the mandate for it. Responsibility is the fulfilment of the obligation that comes with it. Accountability is answerability. For instance, the leader who has the authority to decide on a new policy or product has the responsibility to ensure the team is competent and the process is coordinated well. The leader will be held accountable if the outcome does not meet the required standard. When a leader accepts authority, he must exercise a clear sense of responsibility and accountability. With great power, there must be great responsibility and accountability.

It does not mean that where there is no power, there can be no responsibility. As stated earlier, "Everyone at every level can and must lead." Leadership doesn't mean only to lead down, it also means to lead across and lead up, even when one is "not given the power". There is always the "responsibility" of leading across and leading up, no matter which level you are leading at.

Finally, to implement well, the leader must be able to articulate the vision clearly and forcefully – people must understand why we are doing what we are doing. The vision must be communicated constantly, down to the people in frontline positions and reinforced with rewards. People must take ownership of the vision. Engage, engage and engage.

People Engagement and Development

Why do people join an organisation? First, for the job itself. It must bring a significant sense of purpose to their lives. Second, for career growth. And third, for the pay and benefits. Pay and benefits must be externally competitive and internally equitable.

How does an organisation recruit? It must recruit on the basis of merit. What kind of people does the organisation need? It depends on its purpose. Intellectual capacity is just one ingredient. Skills, both demonstrated and potential, are important. The individual's ability as well as his contribution to the whole team or organisation must be considered. A football team doesn't require every player to be a striker even though scoring goals helps it to win. The team needs strikers, midfielders, defenders and the goalkeeper, not to mention coaches and supporting staff. Diversity and teamwork are important.

Character is paramount. Dee Hock, the founder of Visa Inc., recommends: "Hire and promote first on the basis of integrity; second, motivation; third, capacity; fourth, understanding; fifth, knowledge; and last and least, experience. Without integrity, motivation is dangerous; without motivation, capacity is impotent; without capacity, understanding is limited; without understanding, knowledge is meaningless; without knowledge, experience is blind. Experience is easy to provide and quickly put to good use by people with all the other qualities." Integrity is most important.

And having recruited the people, the organisation needs to provide them with the best environment (training, culture, self-confidence, etc.) to ensure excellence and service.

People need to be engaged. There is a saying: People come for the mission – and they leave because of the manager. The art of engagement will be critical to ensure talent retention, autonomy and efficacy, belonging to organisation and other key enablers of organisational development which will impact longer-term goals and outcomes.

Leaders must, above all, care deeply for their people. They do this by playing the role of teacher, mentor and coach. What is the difference between a teacher, mentor and coach? A teacher delivers structured information, knowledge and ideas. A mentor is an experienced and trusted superior officer who offers advice (often freely and in an unstructured way) in response to a specific need or question by the mentee. The mentor advises and influences the mentee's career. It could be a long-term growth and relationship. A coach listens and asks questions. Insightful questioning (while giving feedback, showing empathy and withholding judgment) can help the individual see himself and the world differently and arrive at his solution.

An educationist once corrected me, saying a teacher does more than teach. I totally agree. My Raffles Institution school friends and I still remember Mr Hector Chee, our Secondary 3/4 maths teacher. He was a teacher, a mentor and a coach. In the late 1960s, he introduced the then new Mathematics Syllabus C with modern maths concepts like set theory, matrices and Venn diagrams that made mathematics interesting and relevant. Mathematics, as taught by him, came alive and was never boring. Through his teaching, many of us improved our logical and creative thinking.

Hector Chee constantly challenged us with difficult problems he had sourced from various places, including those set by the UK examination boards. He also asked us to help him vet the answers to questions he had set for the new mathematics textbook he was writing. We enjoyed the challenge of solving problems without having a model answer to check if we were correct. Sometimes, we suspected that he himself wasn't sure of the answer, so we had to rely on ourselves, be confident that we had applied the concepts correctly and that we had arrived at the correct answers. This motivated us to want to do even better.

Hector Chee's influence went beyond the classroom. We knew he cared for us and we could consult him if we had a problem. He was a teacher whom we respect. Even many years after we left school, he was a person we could relate to and communicate with at ease. He must have taught thousands of students, and yet he could recognise most of us whenever we met him. He always tried his best to attend the Old Rafflesians' Association annual dinners or the class reunions that we organised now and then. He took pride in the success of his students who have done well in their life and career. In 2015, his students set up an RI-Hector Chee Scholarship in his honour. We were glad we launched it and that he was able to grace the occasion. Sadly, he passed away in 2022.

We cannot expect all leaders to be equally good at teaching, mentoring and coaching. Just as the student learns various subjects at different grade levels from different teachers as he progresses in the school system, the individual will have to seek out different leaders to guide him in different stages of his career and life. Even a good leader does not have all the answers. And an outsider can often be an effective coach.

Questions:

- How do you lead?
- How do you get results with people and through people?

CHAPTER 2

Managers and Leaders: Are They Different?

The words manager and leader are often used interchangeably. For example, the Advanced Management Program, which is the top Harvard Business School (HBS) executive programme, has the stated aim to "prepare for the highest level of leadership". The advanced management programme is clearly a senior leadership course. So, are leadership and management different?

Abraham Zaleznik (1924-2011), a Harvard Business School professor, believed that leaders and managers are very different as discussed in his article "Managers and Leaders: Are They Different?" (*Harvard Business Review*, January 2004 reprint, first published 1977).

Zaleznik explained that managers embrace process, seek stability, and control, and instinctively try to resolve problems quickly – sometimes before they fully understand a problem's significance. Leaders, in contrast, tolerate chaos and lack of structure and are willing to delay closure to understand the issues more fully. Managers relate to people according to the role they play in a sequence of events or in a decision-making process. Leaders are concerned with ideas and relate in more intuitive and empathetic ways.

According to Zaleznik, leaders are active instead of reactive, shaping ideas instead of responding to them. Leaders adopt a personal and active attitude towards goals. The influence a leader exerts in altering moods, evoking images, and expectations, and in establishing specific desires and objectives that determine the direction a business takes.

Zaleznik's article makes clear the distinction between a manager's attention to how things get done and a leader's attention to what the events and decisions mean to participants.

Building on the points made in Zaleznik's article, John Kotter, HBS professor of leadership, states in *What Leaders Really Do* (*Harvard Business Review*, December 2001 reprint, first published 1990) that management is about coping with complexity, while leadership is about coping with change. According to Kotter, leaders as opposed to managers are engaged in Setting Direction instead of Planning and Budgeting; Aligning People instead of Organising and Staffing; and Motivating and Inspiring instead of Controlling activities and Solving problems.

Fortuitously, I was exposed to Zaleznik's and Kotter's writings around the time when I was made a department head and a director. I understood that I needed to change and acquire new skills as I moved up the hierarchy. I became more aware of the need to shape ideas and change the way people think about what is desirable, possible and necessary. I also realised that I should not always try to solve problems too quickly to ensure closure, but to spend more time to fully understand the problem and its implications. I needed to move from organising and controlling people and activities to aligning, motivating and developing people. I needed to develop leaders under me, not just get things done. I had to lead change, not just manage complexity.

While it is important to understand the difference between leadership and management, it is even more important to understand that leading and managing are complementary; they are two different roles that require different orientations and skills. An organisation can only perform well and achieve good results if both leadership and management are present. With good management and poor leadership, the team will lack the motivation to pursue goals. Without good management skills, the direction set by a leader risks being unattainable and unsustainable.

I believe that a good leader must both lead and manage. A leader without management skills or the support of a good management team is a disaster. Indeed, each of us needs to be both a leader and manager. We exercise more leadership and less management at higher levels, and more management at lower levels.

Questions:

+ How is leading different from managing?
+ Have you been leading or managing? Or both?

References

Kotter, John. "What Leaders Really Do", *Harvard Business Review*, December 2001.

Zaleznik, Abraham. "Managers and Leaders: Are They Different?", *Harvard Business Review*, January 2004.

CHAPTER 3

Why Do You Want to Be a Leader?

There is a popular Japanese medical drama titled *Doctor-X*. The story revolves around Michiko Daimon (Dr X), a gifted freelance doctor and a maverick, who is interested only in performing surgeries and saving lives, not in hierarchy or job title, amidst the politicking and power play among career doctors in the university hospital. Her success in treating high-risk patients is a result of always putting the patients first, prioritising their health above performing medical firsts or innovative techniques, and adapting the right surgical methods on the spot when needed. This practice often puts her into conflict with other doctors. While this example is based on a television drama, it is relevant to this discussion because it talks about the motivation for leadership – what drives people to the top.

In one episode (*Dr X*, Season 2, Episode 8, 2013), the ambitious Dr Kondo asks Dr X to perform a difficult surgery on a VIP patient on his behalf. Kondo will assist Dr X in the surgery but be credited as the lead surgeon. Kondo will be appointed to the vacant position of department head in the prestigious university hospital if the operation is successful. Although an accomplished surgeon, he is not confident of performing the complicated and high-risk procedure, hence he asks Dr X to help.

Dr X: Why is it so important to you to become the department head?

Kondo: I want to see the view from the top.

What drives people to want to reach for the top, even to the extent of employing dubious means? The motivation could be power, riches, fame, influence or ego. These are not good reasons and in the J-drama, Kondo eventually saw the fruitlessness of his quest and withdrew from the race. However, a real-life Kondo might not have the conscience to do the right thing.

If we want to be a leader for the wrong reasons, we will never be able to lead people to achieve real success, nor will we be truly happy. It is then better to take on "non-leadership" or specialist jobs that could bring success and material rewards.

I often ask my students at the beginning of my course, why do they want to be a leader? Some examples of their responses are provided below.

One student says she wants to be a leader because she would like her country to have a better future. It breaks her heart to see what her country has become with rampant corruption and insatiable greed by those in power. Most of her leaders have failed and many in her country have become disinterested in politics or public service and would prefer to leave the country altogether because the situation feels hopeless. She quotes the saying, "The only thing necessary for the triumph of evil is for good men to do nothing." She doesn't want to do nothing.

She adds that she doesn't consider herself particularly special, at least not in the way leaders are portrayed throughout history, with an almost superhero or saviour-like quality. In fact she professes to have been quite a shy child who, as she grew older, gained confidence and now loves being around people and being able to help them, building relationships and making others happy.

She hopes to be a woman of character and integrity, to lead with both strength and kindness. She wants to learn to be both a better leader and follower, to be able to help make her country a place where her fellow countrymen can be safe, thrive and live with dignity. She wants to do her part and give her best.

This student offered a very powerful statement on why she wants to be a leader. And throughout the semester, I could observe that she had the character and determination to match her words. I wish her and her country the best.

A student from Kazakhstan shared that he had witnessed the negative consequences of nuclear tests and radiation during his time as a volunteer in the villages and suburbs and oncological centres – 456 atomic bombs were tested just 150 kilometres from his hometown between 1949 and 1989. Having experienced this tragic legacy of the Cold War, he wants to play a leading role in his country's diplomacy, foreign policy and governance.

However, not everyone needs to have a grand national perspective.

A student from Western Europe says that his motivation to become a leader is driven by his desire to have a purpose and have a positive contribution to the world, no matter how small or large it may be. He has found inspiration in many different leaders who have given him hope, inspiration and a willingness to act for the good of others rather than simply his own. He wants to be able to inspire people to work for the good of others, and to have the opportunity to help others achieve this objective by providing them with skills and experience.

A student from China says that some of the goals are beyond his individual ability, so teamwork is needed. Effective leadership can help the team perform better. However, if someone can lead the team better than him, he prefers to be one of the followers. Therefore, he does not have to be a leader. He just wants the goal to be achieved better.

An Indonesian student shares that throughout his career, he has learnt that not all superiors are worth being called leaders. He did not feel empowered working for them, and he wants to be a leader who can empower the people around him while getting closer to their objectives.

An Australian student admits she is still finding her purpose. Her reasons for wanting to be a leader is to have the ability to shape work priorities, and to shape decisions.

One Malaysian student confesses she has never wanted to be a leader, nor is she naturally gifted for it. She would rather be a follower; she just wants to be useful and effective. However, in the public service, one would climb up the career ladder as she gains seniority and experience whether she likes it or not. Being a leader is unavoidable, even if only a leader of a smallest team. Because every decision impacts the nation, her team would need to perform well so that people are confident with the public service.

A Singaporean student says that, growing up, she never thought of herself as a leader. She finds it incredibly stressful to be responsible for others. However, her work in the Ministry of Health during the COVID-19 pandemic has changed her perspective on this. In such a crisis, everyone must step up and take charge. She learned that despite, or maybe because of, her avoidance of being a leader, colleagues were more likely to go to her for discussion and even advice. They trusted her to present the final recommendation to their bosses as they felt that she was able to listen and take in various perspectives and present them in a balanced and objective manner. She was also able to translate the bosses' guidance to concrete follow-ups. With this experience, she has started to grow into the shoes of a leader, albeit with much doubt about her ability to become an effective one. She does not have a ground-breaking new vision for the public service; she just wants to continue the good work other leaders have done. She sees every interaction as an opportunity to influence and inspire people around her to learn more about themselves, as well as contribute to the common vision of ensuring all Singaporeans have a chance to succeed in Singapore.

I have listed the nationalities of the students I cited to lend authenticity. But the students are not representative of their nationalities. Students of the same country have a broad spectrum of views towards their country's challenges and their own ambition. What is common in their answers is a fundamental point about leadership: <u>To lead is to serve</u>.

Before we dive into the specifics and technicalities of how to become a better leader, it is important to remember this fundamental principle about leadership. Some individuals who reach leadership positions may feel that they have earned it because they have undergone years of training and trials, service and sacrifice. Or that they have superior intellect and capability, that they are the best people, most capable and most qualified, to lead the organisation and that they deserve recognition and huge rewards. They feel entitled and forget to serve. A leader must always remember to work towards the betterment of others.

We have good reasons to want to be a leader if:

- We have a goal or a dream for a better future for the people and we need to mobilise people to help achieve it.
- We want to change things for the better.
- We have ideas to improve the work environment, and get things done better.
- We like to help other people to grow and be more successful.
- Some or all of the above.

If you value self-interest above serving others, if you are chasing a position instead of a purpose, if you cannot get the job done, then you are not cut out to be a leader.

A leader must deliver results, not for himself, but to make things better for his team. Not everyone can be a leader. Nor is there a need for everyone to be a leader. Some can be specialists. And many can be successful and happy being followers.

But if you want to be a leader, and have the right motivation and ability to be a leader, are you cut out to be a leader?

Questions:

* Why do you want to be a leader?
* When is one a leader? How do you exercise leadership when you are relatively junior?

CHAPTER 4

Can Anyone Be a Leader?

The Center for Creative Leadership conducted research, asking 361 C-level executives "Are leaders born or made?" and found that their views were decidedly mixed.

19% believed that leaders are more born,

52% believed they are more made, and

29% believed that leaders are about equally born *and* made.

As noted in the centre's publication of that research, "Are Leaders Born or Made?" (March 2012), William Gentry and his co-authors found that Born Believers believe leaders' Traits are most important in creating leaders (41%) as against Experience (38%) and Training (21%), while Made Believers place substantially more importance on Experience (46%) and Training (34%) as opposed to Traits (20%).

Does personality determine whether a person is a leader or manager?

How different is the personality of a leader from that of a manager? Abraham Zaleznik refers to the division of personality types made by William James in *The Varieties of Religious Experience* (1902). James describes two basic personality types: "once-born" and "twice-born". Once-borns are those for whom adjustments to life have been straightforward and whose lives have been more or less a peaceful flow since birth. Twice-borns, on the other hand, have not had an easy time of it. Their lives are marked by a continual struggle to attain some sense of order. Unlike once-borns, they cannot take things for granted. According to James, these personalities have equally different world views. For a once-born personality, the sense of self as a guide to conduct and attitude derives from a feeling of being at home and in harmony with one's environment. For a twice-born, the sense of self derives from a feeling of profound separateness.

Zaleznik argues that "managers tend to be once-born personalities. A manager's sense of self-worth is enhanced by perpetuating and strengthening existing institutions: He or she is performing in a role that harmonises with ideals of duty and responsibility. Leaders tend to be twice-born personalities, people who feel separate from their environment. They may work in organisations, but they never belong to them. Their sense of who they are does not depend on memberships, work roles, or other social indicators of identity. And that perception of identity may form the theoretical basis for explaining why certain individuals seek opportunities for change."

Personality may play a role in effective leadership, but we have the ability to manage our personality. Even Zaleznik accepts that leadership can be developed.

Zaleznik examines two types of leadership development: (1) development through socialisation, which prepares the individual to guide institutions and maintain the existing balance of social relations; and (2) development through personal mastery, which impels an individual to struggle for psychological and social change. His view is that society produces its managerial talent through the first line of development; leaders emerge through the second.

Zaleznik postulates that one-on-one relationships are the key to developing leadership in an organisation. Psychological biographies of gifted people repeatedly demonstrate the important part a teacher plays in developing an individual. Dwight D. Eisenhower writes in his autobiography *At Ease: Stories I Tell to Friends*: "Life with General Connor was a sort of graduate school in military affairs and the humanities, leavened by a man who was experienced in his knowledge of men and their conduct. I can never adequately express my gratitude to this one gentleman. ...In a lifetime of association with great and good men, he is the one more or less invisible figure to whom I owe an incalculable debt." Before General Fox Conner, Eisenhower's military career was very mediocre. But the magnificent tutorial he received under Conner changed him. He went on to graduate first in his class at the US Command and General Staff Course, and excelled in various command and staff postings thereafter.

I have had the good fortune of working with many good bosses throughout my career. I was very mediocre during my basic military training and officer cadet training. As a young officer posted to an infantry battalion upon graduation from university, I learned much from the company commanders and especially the battalion commander, a Commando officer who was promoted to Major at age 23, and who did chin-ups with one arm and tolerated no nonsense from the soldiers as well as officers. Later I served under another battalion commander who had topped the Command and Staff Course. I learned from them how to lead men, manage a unit as well as deploy army tactics. I began to do well in basic and advanced officers' courses and even topped the Command and Staff Course. I later learned much on public policy analysis and formulation and public service delivery from Mr Lim Siong Guan, who was my Permanent Secretary in the Ministry of Defence, and again as my Permanent Secretary in the Ministry of Finance when I was the Deputy Secretary (Revenue) and Deputy Secretary (Policy). I also had the opportunity to learn from Mr Goh Chok Tong when I worked as his Military Personal Secretary when he was the Minister for Defence, and later as his Principal Private Secretary when he was Prime Minister. Of course, we don't always have good bosses, but we can learn from bad bosses too. As Confucius says: 三人行, 必有我师. It means (as translated by James Legge): "When I walk along with two others, they may serve me as my teachers. I will select their good qualities and follow them, their bad qualities and avoid them."

I was also fortunate to have many outstanding officers working with and under me in the various ministries and statutory boards. I had spent much effort to mentor and coach some of them because I saw their talents and potential.

Whether gifted individuals find what they need in one-to-one relationships depends on the availability of great teachers. And as Zaleznik writes, great teachers take risks. They bet initially on talent they perceive in younger people. And they risk emotional involvement in working closely with their juniors. The risks do not always pay off, but the willingness to take them appears to be crucial in developing leaders.

The key point to note is: Personality can be managed and leadership skills can be taught.

In fact, leadership must be taught.

In Henry Kissinger's book *Leadership: Six Studies in World Strategy* (Penguin, 2022), about six leaders whom he considered having a motivating vision and the character, intellect and hardiness to deal with world order (Konrad Adenauer, Charles de Gaulle, Richard Nixon, Anwar Sadat, Lee Kuan Yew and Margaret Thatcher), he writes:

"As we have seen, leaders with world-historical impact have benefited from a rigorous and humanistic education. Such an education begins

in a formal setting and continues for a lifetime through reading and discussion with others. That initial step is rarely taken today – few universities offer an education in statecraft either explicitly or implicitly – and the lifelong effort is made more difficult as changes in technology erode literacy. Thus, for meritocracy to be reinvigorated, humanistic education would need to regain its significance, embracing such subjects as philosophy, politics, human geography, modern languages, history, economic thought, literature and even, perhaps, classical antiquity, the study of which was long the nursery of statesmen."

(Comment: Kissinger cited classical antiquity which is the Greco-Roman era, but an understanding of a similar period in China [Lao Tzu and Confucius; Qin, Han and Tang Dynasties], the Middle East and India are similarly relevant. Culture which is the foundation for politics, philosophy, literature, law, education, etc., is important.)

Barbara Kellerman (Founding Executive Director of the Center for Public Leadership at the Harvard Kennedy School), posted on 15 August 2022 the above Kissinger quote to argue for a far, far more rigorous, and broad-based process by which leaders should be educated, trained and developed. She concludes: "How quaint is Kissinger – and how right. We get the leaders we deserve because we do not raise them right. Until we raise them – educate them, train them, and develop them – as we do our doctors and lawyers and teachers and engineers, we will be stuck with far too many leaders who are second and third rate or, heaven forefend, worse. Sad – first rate leaders should not be by accident, they should be by design."

It is also important to note that the exercise of leadership is not reserved for the very top. Do not wait till you are at the top, in a so-called leadership position. Every one of us at every level must exercise leadership. Our responsibility and authority may vary, but each one of us can make a difference. We can all improve our organisation within our scope and capability. We must each take ownership of the organisation we are a member of.

Questions:

* Are leaders born or made?
* If you want to be a leader, and have the right motivation to be a leader, how can you become one?
* How different is public service leadership from leadership in the private sector?

References

Zaleznik, Abraham. "Managers and Leaders: Are They Different?", *Harvard Business Review*, January 2004.

Short Thoughts on Leadership

Lim Siong Guan

I was on my way to speak at a conference when the organiser asked me late in the evening before to summarise my thoughts on leadership in less than 10 words.

It seemed to me to be such a preposterous last-minute request. Nevertheless, when I awoke the next morning, I had my answer, six words in three phrases: "Think People, Think Future, Think Excellence". Every thought I had on leadership could fit into one of the three aspects.

Thinking People seemed to be such a natural imperative. Do unto others as you would have them do unto you! The people you interact with are never digits or toys to push around. They are sensitive beings who seek to be appreciated and respected.

Thinking Future is a critical demand which, it seems to me, many CEOs appear to be able to get away with not doing. Yet preparing their people and positioning the organisation for survivability and sustainable success is the one responsibility which is uniquely theirs. Nevertheless, if a crisis does not strike in their time which would expose their neglect, they could well get away with it. When the tide runs out, it has been said, you will see who has been swimming naked. But there are lucky people who are not there when the tide runs out.

Finally, Thinking Excellence! I do not use the word "excellence" to mean "outstanding". I mean it to be "being the best you can be" where performance reflects potential, nothing less though it can never be more.

Allow me to elaborate on these points.

Think People

Laozi, one of the three philosophy greats of China, had said,

> *"As for the best leaders, the people do not notice their existence. The next best, the people honour and praise. The next, the people fear; and the next, the people hate. When the best leader's work is done, his aim fulfilled, the people will say, 'We did it ourselves?'"*

Our hearts' desires should be to help our people realise their talents and abilities to the greatest extent possible. We should want our people to be full of self-confidence, proud of themselves and fully committed to the task at hand.

Every leader needs to have the heart of a teacher. Teaching is a truly unique vocation. It is to help every student be the best they can be. For many situations in the office or the factory, the leader seeks to stay on top as the way of success. Yet for the teacher, the student exceeding him or her in later life is the measure of success; the more the student succeeds, the greater the teacher's success.

To me, the most important question a leader must continually ask is, "How can I help you do your job better?"

The first "you" is your boss – help him or her succeed! This is how you build up their trust in you.

The second "you" is your peers – help them succeed! They will be more prepared to help you in return, or at least be less likely to sabotage you.

And the third "you" is, of course, the people who serve under you.

When I was in the Ministry of Finance many years ago, I wanted to develop a formula of sorts to help my managers succeed as leaders. A couple of my lady officers volunteered to work out such a formula for me.

Some weeks later, they came to me with their solution, which I welcomed as being simply brilliant. What people want of their supervisors, they told me, is for them to practise "GEESE":

G is to have the willingness to Teach and the ability to Guide.

E is to have the capacity to Empathise, to feel with and for their People.

E again is to Energise their People to push themselves to maximum Performance.

S is to Synergise the efforts of their many people so that 1 plus 1 can be more than 2.

E is to Embolden their People to Think and Try innovative and creative ways to better get things done.

"GEESE" seems simple enough as a formula for good leadership. The challenge is to do it with your whole heart and mind, so your people know you are not putting up a show but that this is the genuine you.

Think Future

There is an African proverb which says, "Every day the gazelle wakes up knowing that if it can't outrun the fastest lion, it's going to be somebody's breakfast. And every day the lion wakes up knowing that if it can't outrun the slowest gazelle it will go hungry." If you can imagine the African safari, you can imagine the truth of the proverb.

What do you imagine yourself to be, the lion or the gazelle?

It would be facetious to say, "It doesn't matter whether you are the lion or the gazelle; when the sun comes up, you had better be running!"

But it does matter a lot whether you imagine yourself to be the lion or the gazelle.

If you were the lion, you would need to make sure you have the muscle and stamina to keep up with the gazelle. And all you need do is to follow the gazelle whichever way it chooses to run.

If you were the gazelle, not only would you need to have the muscle and the stamina to outlast the lion. Your brain should be ticking all the time to try to find a path which would be more difficult for the lion to follow you.

Running as the gazelle needs an active and alert mind, while running as the lion is to have the mind of the follower.

Looking back on the COVID-19 pandemic, I think the greatest lesson we should take from it is to prepare ourselves to survive and do well in a future of Unknown Unknowns. I know Nassim Nicholas Taleb, esteemed author of *The Black Swan*, has said that we cannot say the pandemic was a black swan event; it was not unexpected and many people had predicted the event of a pandemic. But, to me, the last time the world had a global pandemic was the Spanish Flu, 100 years ago. COVID-19 struck us largely as an unknown unknown, despite its similarities to SARS, severe acute respiratory syndrome, which struck from 2002 to 2004.

If the future were completely Known, we will know what best to do and we can prepare ourselves the best way possible for every situation. And if the future were Unknown, but we know what the Unknowns are, we can prepare ourselves by developing a series of plausible futures, a technique known as scenario-based planning. It is possible to prepare plans and actions ahead of time when we know what we do not know.

But what can we do when we do not know what we do not know, the future of Unknown Unknowns.

Rosabeth Moss Kanter is a professor of business at Harvard Business School. She has made the observation that financial results are a "lagging indicator" of a company's health. "They tell you what you've just done (or had failed to do). They don't predict the future." (See Dina Gerdeman, "Why Uber is Worth Saving and How to Do It", *HBS Research & Ideas,* 29 June 2017.)

She adds, "Culture is a leading indicator. Culture predicts the future." Indeed, she asserts, "culture…(is) more important in some ways than strategy."

And finally, she made the remark that should make every leader sit up: "If you're not thinking about building your culture for survivability and sustainability, then you're not leading."

This, to me, is the most important point about how to keep

winning in an unpredictable future. It is to build a culture for survivability and sustainability.

Culture is that collection of values and beliefs needed to produce the behaviours we believe to be critical for winning. Culture is the ultimate competitive advantage – we can buy expertise, we can buy technology, but we cannot buy the winning culture because it lives in the hearts and minds of the people in the winning organisation.

Yet the winning culture does not exist in a vacuum – it is not a collection of ideals you decide to pull out of books or articles on leadership. The culture you need depends on the future you want to get to. The clearer you are in your vision, the stronger your conviction on the culture you need to build.

Think Excellence

In chasing productivity, we can think in terms of going from Efficiency to Effectiveness to Excellence.

Efficiency is to get more Output for each unit of Input. It is the ratio of Output to Input, for example, you may wish to measure efficiency in a hospital by way of bed occupancy, the percentage of beds occupied by patients.

Effectiveness is to focus on Outcomes in comparison to the Resources committed. Thus, for a hospital, the measure of outcome could be the percentage of patients cured of the sickness they had arrived at the hospital with. Patients go to hospitals because they are sick: We should measure the hospital's effectiveness in terms of patients healed of their sickness.

But the most fundamental of measures of productivity should be Performance achieved as compared to the Potential, meaning what is potentially possible given the human, infrastructure and financial resources available. I refer to this as Driving for Excellence. While the measurement of Performance may be straightforward, measurement of Potential would be more difficult because Potential should be going up with time and experience. Thus the measure of Excellence should be considered as dropping if Performance remains unchanged despite experience gained with time. In reality, Excellence should be seen more as a way of thinking – a perspective, approach and attitude – rather than a numerical measure.

We have to address six factors in the pursuit of Excellence.

First, our people should be doing the best they can. This is a *morale* and *motivation* issue. How do we keep up morale? How do we keep enhancing motivation?

Second, our people should be the best they can be. This is a *capacity* and *capability* issue. Do we have a good talent management system, where we seek to identify talent – defined as the highest level a worker could be expected to reach by the time they retire – as early as possible, so that we may gain maximum time benefit from what they are capable, while they derive maximum motivation through the opportunity to be recognised, to learn, improve, contribute, and display and exercise what they are capable of?

Third, our people should see their performance being enhanced by your capacity for *synergy* and *symbiosis*. Synergy is to successfully get maximum effect from your people working well together in their work teams, and maximum value from your work units and departments working together in united purpose and coherent effort.

Synergy is where 1 plus 1 yields more than 2, where the whole is more than the sum of the parts. Symbiosis is where your people and their work units interact with each other to the advantage of both in producing useful and beneficial results not possible if they had not joined together in mutual support.

The Final Word

So there you have it: The unending challenge of leadership is to *think people, think future, think excellence.*

And all to a common end: *Leadership is making good things happen that on their own would not happen.*

ABOUT LIM SIONG GUAN

Lim Siong Guan was the Head of the Singapore Civil Service from September 1999 to March 2005. He had been the Permanent Secretary of the Ministry of Defence, and served in the Prime Minister's Office, the Ministry of Education and the Ministry of Finance. He was the first Principal Private Secretary to the founding Prime Minister Lee Kuan Yew. He has chaired the Central Provident Fund Board, Inland Revenue Authority of Singapore and Singapore Economic Development Board. He was Group President of GIC, Singapore's sovereign wealth fund, from 2007 to 2016. He has been a professor of practice at the Lee Kuan Yew School of Public Policy of the National University of Singapore, and lectures frequently on leadership, change management and preparing for the future. Lim Siong Guan and co-author Joanne H. Lim wrote the book *The Leader, The Teacher & You* (Singapore: World Scientific, 2013).

PART

2

LEADING BETTER WITH THE 5Cs

Clarity
Courage
Communication
Caring-ness
Culture

From observation, reading and experience, I find that a leader will lead well by adopting the 5Cs of the Leadership Framework. The 5Cs are not traits. They are not idiosyncrasies. They are actions that a leader must do to lead effectively.

The 5Cs are:

1. Clarity. To have clarity, we start by asking ourselves: Why am I here? Why would people follow me? To achieve clarity, we must make sense of the world around us, have foresight and make good decisions.

2. Courage. Courage is overcoming our fear. Courage is important because a leader makes decisions, leads change and needs to be resilient in the face of adversity.

3. Communication. Communication is particularly important in public service leadership, because leaders have to communicate at different levels and to different groups of citizens with different needs, concerns and biases.

4. Caring-ness. To lead is to serve. People don't care how much you know, until they know how much you care.

5. Culture. Culture is vital to sustaining organisational and societal values. Culture eats strategy for breakfast.

The 5Cs must be incorporated in a consistent and authentic way. The leader must have, above all else, good character.

Part 2 contains seven chapters and six essays. Ambassador Tommy Koh's short elegant essay on "How to Be a Good Leader" shares rules that he has observed for himself in his work. Chua Chin Kiat's "Musings on Leadership" is based on his experience as Director of the Singapore Prison Service, which he helped transform from a custody-focused mindset to a rehabilitation-centred culture. Yanuar Nugroho, Deputy

Chief of Staff to the President of Indonesia from 2015 to 2019, writes about the challenges in reforming the Indonesian bureaucracy. The essay by Pum Huot, Personal Advisor to the Prime Minister of Cambodia, is titled "Leadership During Changes", with specific reference to the leadership transition in Cambodia. Kelvin Lester K. Lee, former Commissioner of the Philippine Securities and Exchange Commission, writes about "Leadership Lessons in the Digital Transformation of the Philippine SEC". My essay is about how the Singapore Urban Redevelopment Authority, taking into account public feedback, "saved" Chek Jawa.

CHAPTER 5

Clarity

To have clarity of mind, purpose and direction, we start by asking ourselves: Why am I here?

Why Am I Here?

Whenever you are posted to a new job or assigned a new responsibility, ask yourself: What is the job? What is its purpose? What am I expected to accomplish? How is success measured?

Clarity is most important. Without clarity, we may run around like clowns.

How does one achieve clarity? First, we must make sense of the world around us. Second, we need to have foresight, the ability to anticipate and see change coming, adapt and act. Scenario planning is a good tool to help us gain foresight. Third, we need to make good decisions.

Sense-making

MIT professor Deborah Ancona et al. wrote ("The Overlooked Key to Leading Through Chaos", *MIT Sloan Management Review*, Fall 2020) that the one critical capability that leaders need most in turbulent times is sense-making, a term introduced by organisational psychologist Karl Weick in 1969 that has been recognised as vital to the success and survival of organisations since. According to Ancona, sense-making involves:

- Pulling together disparate views to create a plausible understanding of the complexity around us; and then,
- Testing that understanding to refine it or, if necessary, abandon it and start over.

Weick likened the process of sense-making to cartography. What we map depends on where we look, what factors we choose to focus on and what aspects of the terrain we decide to represent. Since these choices will shape the kind of map we produce, there is no perfect map of a terrain. Therefore, making sense is more than an act of analysis; it's an act of creativity.

Christopher Columbus made landfall in the Americas in October 1492; his landing place was an island in the Bahamas. He thought he had arrived in the Indies, an old name for Asia. Did he have a map? Yes, it was a 1491 map of the world, created by the German cartographer Henricus Martellus. Was it accurate? Its depiction of Europe and the Mediterranean were more or less accurate, but not so for the rest of the world. In fact, the map led Columbus to believe he had reached Asia when he had landed in the Bahamas because it did not show that another continent lay in front of him. Nevertheless, Columbus is hailed as the first explorer to establish a European presence in the New World. Columbus might have mistaken America for Asia. But without a map, he probably would not have set sail. To quote Columbus (1492):

"Following the light of the sun, we left the Old World. By prevailing over all obstacles and distractions, one may unfailingly arrive at his chosen goal or destination."

(cited in John Sase, "Expert Witness", *LegalNews*, 16 November 2011).

We must be mindful that the map we hold could be wrong; we should be on the lookout for signs and signals to update and adjust our map accordingly: obtain data from multiple sources, involve others and be open to new possibilities. Leaders need to have a wide network, listen, see patterns in complexity, be open to new ideas and be able to rapidly test their assumptions. The ability to discern and synthesise, and to take on multiple perspectives is important.

The ability to take in a welter of information and transform it into something clear is increasingly important. Indeed, Howard Gardner (Harvard Professor of Education, known for his theory of multiple intelligences , in *Five Minds for the Future* [2009]), calls the synthesising mind the most important of the five minds that must be cultivated for success in the future. The others include:

- Disciplined mind: the disciplined mind masters one or more ways of thinking used in a discipline or profession. "Be prepared to be an expert in something," said Gardner, and to sustain that learning for life.

- Creating mind: the creating mind challenges old ideas, uncovers fresh ways of thinking, and requires a "robust, iconoclastic temperament," Gardner said. But the creating mind must first master one or more disciplines, and synthesise what is already known.

- Respectful mind: the respectful mind learns tolerance for those who are different, and devises ways to understand and get along with others. "The respectful mind respects diversity as a fact of life," said Gardner, and goes beyond "mere tolerance".
- Ethical mind: the ethical mind takes a step back from the self and considers the needs of society.

All five minds are important and should be cultivated, but to Gardner, "Skill at synthesizing is becoming an imperative for the new millennium. Those who can synthesize well will be valued; those who cannot, will have to rely on the syntheses of others, and may be consigned to the lower end of the occupational and economic ladders."

Gardner continued: "A leader does not have to be a master of everything but he must be able to take on multi-perspectives." "Interdisciplinarity" is when the individual is expected to have achieved significant mastery of more than one discipline – a daunting assignment. "Multi-perspectivalism" is when the individual picks up enough of the approach so that he can follow discussions and eventually participate in them; but there is no requirement that he has independent mastery of each discipline.

Foresight

We cannot forecast the future, but some people are better at it. Philip Tetlock and Barbara Mellers at the University of Pennsylvania led a team that topped a huge forecasting tournament run by IARPA (Intelligence Advanced Research Projects Activity) in 2011 for the public. Thousands of contestants, including ordinary Joes and Janes as well as intelligence analysts, were asked to answer about 500 questions, such as: Will North Korea launch a new multistage missile before

10 May 2014? Will Robert Mugabe cease to be president of Zimbabwe by 30 September 2011? The winning team, called the Good Judgment Project, was so accurate that they even outperformed intelligence analysts with access to classified data.

Tetlock concluded that successful forecasters tend to possess the following qualities:

- Intellectual capacity

- Open-mindedness: "You need to change your mind fast, and often"; "how well you deal with uncertainty, are able to see problems from all sides, overcome your preconceptions in the light of new evidence".

- Self-awareness: humility and a willingness to learn from your mistakes; understanding your own foibles.

Teamwork helps. Assembling the most successful forecasters into teams who were able to discuss and argue produced better predictions. Research shows that harnessing a blend of statistics, psychology, training and various levels of interaction between individual forecasters consistently produced the best forecast. Diversity is important. (See Tetlock & Gardner, 2015; also Shoemaker & Tetlock, 2016).

Hedgehog or Fox

Interestingly, Tetlock observes that "low scorers in forecasting look like hedgehogs", while "high scorers in forecasting look like foxes".

Hedgehogs:

- Are thinkers who "know one big thing"

- Aggressively extend the explanatory reach of that one big thing into new domains

- Display bristly impatience with those who "do not get it"
- Express considerable confidence that they are already proficient forecasters, at least in the long term

Foxes:

- Are thinkers who know many small things (tricks of their trade)
- Are sceptical of grand schemes
- See explanation and prediction not as deductive exercises but rather as exercises in flexible "ad hoc-ery" that require stitching together diverse sources of information
- Are rather diffident about their own forecasting prowess
- Are rather dubious that the cloud-like subject of politics can be the object of a clocklike science

Tetlock thinks that "hedgehoggery" is valuable if handled correctly. Hedgehogs provide a valuable service by doing the deep thinking necessary to build detailed causal models and raise interesting questions. These models and questions can then be slurped up by foxy superforecasters, evaluated and aggregated to make good predictions.

Question: Are you a hedgehog or a fox? Which is better?

Scenario Planning

The organisation and people must be able to sense the changing environment, adapt and act. Scenario planning is a structured way for organisations to think about the future. It helped Royal Dutch Shell to act quickly during the oil shock of the early 1970s. In 1991, I was given the opportunity to be attached to Royal Dutch Shell Group Planning as part of the scenario team. On my return, I helped introduce scenario planning to the Singapore Civil Service and the Ministry of Defence. (Scenario Planning is explained in greater details in Chapter 5.1.)

Decision-making

Clarity requires focused pursuit of the vision and good decision-making.

How do leaders make good decisions? Peter Drucker explains that it is important to define the right problem(s) and ask the right questions. In "What We Can Learn from Japanese Management", *Harvard Business Review*, March 1971, Drucker writes:

> ".... the Westerner and the Japanese mean something different when they talk of 'making a decision'. With us in the West, all the emphasis is on the answer to the question. Indeed, our books on decision making try to develop systematic approaches to giving an answer. To the Japanese, however, the important element in decision making is defining the question. The important and crucial steps are to decide whether there is a need for a decision and what the decision is about. And it is in this step that the Japanese aim at attaining 'consensus'. Indeed, it is this step that, to the Japanese, is the essence of the decision. The answer to the question (what the West considers the decision) follows its definition.*

> "During this process that precedes the decision, no mention is made of what the answer might be. This is done so that people will not be forced to take sides; once they have taken sides, a decision would be a victory for one side and a defeat for the other. Thus, the whole process is focused on finding out what the decision is really about,*

not what the decision should be. Its result is a meeting of the minds that there is (or is not) a need for a change in behaviour."

Defining the right problem requires us to consider the strategic dimension of a project or policy proposal before deciding on its cost benefit:

- What is the case for change or intervention?
- What outcomes are expected?
- How do these fit with wider organisation policies and objectives?

Focus and prioritisation are important. The 80–20 rule (also known as the Pareto principle, which states that for many outcomes, roughly 80% of consequences come from 20% of causes) can help good decision-making by focusing on the important decisions needed, the approximately 20% of our efforts that produce 80% of the results. Named after the Italian economist Vilfredo Pareto who showed in 1906 that approximately 80% of the land in the Kingdom of Italy was owned by 20% of the population, the principle has now been applied to many areas such as business, economics, health and technology. Of course, we must be aware that not all populations follow the 80–20 rule.

We are also required to consider the Public Communication Dimension early. How will the public receive the proposal? What is the communication plan? Public Communication is an integral part of decision-making and should not be an afterthought.

The leader should seek diversity of opinions and information to avoid an echo chamber and groupthink that reinforce what we think is true.

Groupthink is a psychological phenomenon that occurs within a group of people, in which the desire for harmony or conformity in the group results in an irrational or dysfunctional decision-making outcome. (Irving Janis, a Yale research psychologist and later Professor Emeritus at UC Berkeley, conducted much pioneering research on this subject.)

Groupthink will minimise conflict but result in reaching a consensus decision without critical evaluation of alternative viewpoints. It actively suppresses dissenting viewpoints, isolating the group from outside influences.

Thus, there is loss of individual creativity, uniqueness and independent thinking. The "ingroup" produces an "illusion of invulnerability" (an inflated certainty that the right decision has been made), significantly overrates its own abilities in decision-making and significantly underrates the abilities of its opponents (the "outgroup").

A classic example of groupthink lies in the decision-making of the Bay of Pigs Invasion on 17 April 1961, when 1,500 US(CIA)-trained Cubans, called Brigade 2506, landed in Cuba intending to overthrow the increasingly Communist government of Fidel Castro. By 19 April 1961, the Cuban Government had captured or killed the invading exiles, and US President John F. Kennedy (JFK) was forced to negotiate for the release of the 1,189 survivors. After 20 months, Cuba released the captured exiles in exchange for $53 million worth of food and medicine.

The invasion plan was initiated by the Eisenhower administration, but when the Kennedy White House took over (Kennedy became president only on 20 January 1961), it "uncritically accepted" the CIA's plan. When some of Kennedy's advisors, such as Arthur M. Schlesinger, Jr. and Senator J. William Fulbright, attempted to present their objections to the plan, the team as a whole ignored these objections and kept believing in the morality of its plan. According to Schlesinger, he eventually minimised his own doubts, performing self-censorship. The Kennedy team stereotyped Castro and the Cubans by failing to question the CIA about its many false assumptions, including the ineffectiveness of Castro's Air Force, the weakness of Castro's Army and the inability of Castro to quell internal uprisings.

After the experience, JFK (1968) told his journalist friend Ben Bradlee: "The first advice I am going to give to my successor is to watch the generals and to avoid feeling that because they were military men their opinions on military matters were worth a damn."

Joe Biden on the other hand strongly rejected the generals' views when debating the US military exit from Afghanistan. According to *The New York Times* (19 April 2021), the military leadership hoped it could convince the new president to maintain a modest troop presence, but Biden could not be persuaded. There would be no conditions put on the withdrawal. Zero means zero. Barack Obama recalled in his memoir that Biden as his vice president had warned him about "generals who are trying to box in a new President. Don't let them jam you." The result was a chaotic withdrawal and Afghanistan fell quickly to the Talibans. *The Economist* (21-27 August 2021 issue) had the words "BIDEN's DEBACLE" printed in bold on its cover. Its leading article described the "shambolic withdrawal" and the "fiasco in Afghanistan" as a huge and unnecessary blow to America's standing.

So, do leaders listen or not listen to experts? The answer is experts advise and leaders must lead.

The decision process must be clear and avoid groupthink. At Intel, as its former CEO Andrew Grove (1998) likes to tell it, "We developed a style of ferociously arguing with one another while remaining friends (we call this 'constructive confrontation')". Knowledge power trumps position power.

David Garvin and Michael Roberto recommended in "What You Don't Know About Making Decisions" (*Harvard Business Review*, September 2001) that the decision process should seek to encourage inquiry over advocacy.

Advocacy is a contest of persuasion and lobbying: strive to persuade others, defend your position, downplay weaknesses; discourage minority views. The outcome is winners and losers.

Inquiry is collaborative problem solving: testing and evaluation; critical thinking; presenting balanced arguments; open to alternatives; accepting constructive criticism; minority views are cultivated and valued. The outcome is collective ownership.

JFK revised his decision-making process after the Bay of Pigs fiasco. The following decision-making process was used in the Cuban Missile Crisis the following year:

- Free, unstructured discussion
- Team A versus Team B working on alternate plans
- Plans debated without the president's attendance, to avoid people simply following the president's views
- Joint proposal to the president

The Cuban Missile Crisis was a 13-day (16-28 October 1962) confrontation between the United States and the Soviet Union over Soviet ballistic missiles deployed in Cuba. This crisis brought the world closer to nuclear war than at any point before or since, until perhaps now with the Russo-Ukrainian War. The US had no plan in place because US intelligence had been convinced that the Soviets would never install nuclear missiles in Cuba. The Joint Chiefs of Staff unanimously agreed that a full-scale attack and invasion was the only solution. They believed that the Soviets would not attempt to stop the US from conquering Cuba. President Kennedy (1968) was sceptical: "They, no more than we, can let these things go by without doing something. They can't, after all their statements, permit us to take out their missiles, kill a lot of Russians, and then do nothing. If they don't take action in Cuba, they certainly will in Berlin." Kennedy challenged military leaders who pressured him to bomb and invade. He heard the CIA's case for air strikes and Adlai Stevenson's (US Ambassador to the United Nations) counsel for negotiation. Advocates for different views developed their arguments in committees then met back together. The account is described in Robert Kennedy's book, *Thirteen Days*, with a new Foreword by Arthur Schlesinger Jr. and Afterword by Richard Neustadt and Graham Allison.

Of course the truth was more complex. There was negotiation for US withdrawal of missiles from Turkey as quid pro quo. And nuclear war was only avoided because Vasily Arkhipov, the executive officer of a Soviet submarine, refused to authorise the captain's and political officer's use of nuclear torpedoes against the US Navy, a decision requiring the agreement of all three of them.

To avoid groupthink, the team should:

- Comprise diversity, intellectual and ideological
- Be open (and listen) to diverse views, inside and outside the organisation
- Be willing to engage in constructive confrontation
- Encourage inquiry over advocacy.

Daniel Kahneman suggested one way organisations can try to overcome groupthink is by giving them permission to search for potential problems they might be overlooking, citing psychologist

Gary Klein's "premortem" method. To use the method, an organisation would gather its team before making a final decision on an important matter. Then, all the team members are asked to imagine that the decision led to disastrous failure, and to write up why it was a disaster.

The leader should also avoid falling into the CEO Disease. This is the isolation/information vacuum that envelops a leader when subordinates become reluctant to disclose bad news or worst-case scenarios that might trigger a shoot-the-messenger response. It leaves the leader out of touch and out of tune.

Manfred Kets de Vries' (psychoanalyst, consultant and INSEAD professor of leadership) solution to the CEO Disease is that every leader needs a fool. When asked who (the chairman, their best friend?), his answer was, "Your wife, your husband. And the fool should tell you you're full of shit on a regular basis." On consultants, his answer is: "Never hire a hungry consultant. Never." Why? Because they will tell you what you want to hear. (*Financial Times Weekend*, 6-7 March 2001, Lunch with FT, Michael Skapinker)

Leaders need to be able to handle uncertainty and self-doubt. Over-confidence leads to unacceptable risk taking. Pride goes before a fall.

Clarity is not certainty. It helps us to deal with uncertainty. It requires sense-making and foresight; coming up with a vision that motivates. It requires working out options and strategies and showing the pathway towards the vision, and implementing the strategy to achieve the vision.

Take the example of Singapore's water story. During independence in 1965, Singapore relied heavily on imported water from Malaysia. Then Prime Minister Lee Kuan Yew was clear that water security is central to Singapore's existence: "This dominated every other policy. Every other policy had to bend at the knees for water survival."

There was great uncertainty but Lee Kuan Yew's clarity enabled the Public Utilities Board (PUB, the national water agency) and the Ministry of the Environment to deal with the uncertainty. PUB began diversifying Singapore's water supply to include four national taps. These are (i) local catchment water; (ii) imported water from Malaysia; (iii) NEWater, which is treated used water; and (iv) desalinated water. Initially, the foremost water supply challenge was one of increasing the yield from local catchment. Singapore was faced with limited land, absence of large river systems and limited groundwater. Singapore overcame its land constraints through long-term integrated land-use planning. Water catchment and drainage considerations are included in urban planning processes, which also take into account transport, housing and industrial needs. The need to balance competing land needs later led to the creation of unprotected catchments, which enabled urbanised areas to be used as water catchments.

Singapore set very clear short-, medium- and long-term strategies and deliverables. In the 1960s and 1970s, the Singapore River was not the picturesque water body it is today. In 1977, PM Lee declared: "It should be a way of life to keep the water clean, to keep every stream free from unnecessary pollution. In ten years, let us have fishing in the Singapore River and in the Kallang River. It can be done." Ten years later, the clean-up was completed. The job was challenging: The rivers had become very polluted by the 1960s and their combined water catchments covered about one-fifth of the total land area of Singapore. It required massive resettlement of farms, industries and unsewered squatters, and development of infrastructure such as housing, industrial workshops and sewage systems to transform the previously polluted river. The man placed in charge was Mr Lee Ek Tieng, Permanent Secretary for the Environment (and concurrently Chairman of PUB).

Implementation required not only the Environment Ministry but also joint efforts of the Urban Redevelopment Authority (URA), Public Works Department (PWD), Housing and Development Board (HDB), Port of Singapore Authority (PSA) and the Primary Production Department (PPD). Being the right man for the job, and with clear authority, responsibility and accountability, Lee Ek Tieng successfully completed the mission. He was later appointed Head of Civil Service.

PM Lee then issued a new challenge to PUB: "In 20 years, it is possible that there could be breakthroughs in technology, both anti-pollution and filtration, and then we dam up or put a barrage at the mouth of the Marina and we will have a huge freshwater lake… a large strategic reserve of freshwater." Marina Barrage was completed in 2008 and Marina Reservoir was commissioned as a freshwater reservoir in 2010. At the same time, the URA was working to shape the Marina Bay area into the city centre it is today.

Singapore invested heavily in research and technology to address its water needs: microfiltration and reverse osmosis to treat used water and desalt seawater to produce NEWater and desalinated water, respectively. It also implemented the Deep Tunnel Sewerage System to collect, treat, reclaim and dispose of Singapore's used water efficiently and cost effectively, and low-energy electrochemical desalting technologies. Such investments in the water sector have been the seeds for the creation of a new pillar of economic growth for Singapore. To further create opportunities for sharing and co-creation of solutions to address global water challenges, the Singapore International Water Week (SIWW) was established. SIWW has become a successful platform in bringing together decision makers, businesses and researchers to share knowledge, showcase technologies, discover opportunities and celebrate achievements in the water world.

In summary, Singapore leaders take the following actions to achieve clarity in the water challenge:

- Understand the situation and the challenges
- Define a clear vision, organisational mission, goals and objectives
- Take a long-term perspective
- Develop short-, medium- and long-term strategies and key deliverables to create a strong sense of direction
- Be open to all possibilities and be alert to changes in the market and technology
- Take on multi-perspectives
- Assign clear authority, accountability and responsibility
- Ensure results are measurable
- Conduct self-review, post-mortem and pre-mortem regularly

Questions:

- Is a wrong map better than no map?
- How do you ask the right questions in order to decide what the decision is about?
- How to avoid groupthink?
- How do you achieve clarity in tackling a complex challenge?

References

Garvin, David and Michael Roberto. "What You Don't Know About Making Decisions". *Harvard Business Review*, September 2001.

Grove, Andrew S. *Only the Paranoid Survive*. London: Profile Business, 1998.

Hammond, John, Ralph Keeney and Howard Raiffa. "The Hidden Traps in Decision Making". *Harvard Business Review*, January 2006 (originally 1998).

Kahneman, Daniel. *Thinking, Fast and Slow*. New York: FSG, 2011.

Kennedy, John F. *Thirteen Days: A Memoir of the Cuban Missile Crisis*. New York: Norton, 1968, new edition 1999.

Shoemaker, Paul and Philip Tetlock. "Superforecasting: How to Upgrade Your Company's Judgment". *Harvard Business Review*, May 2016.

Tetlock, Philip and Dan Gardner. *Superforecasting: The Art and Science of Prediction*. New York: Crown Publishers, 2015.

Notes on Scenario Planning

T he world is full of uncertainties. Who could have predicted 9/11 (2001), SARS (2002-2003), the global financial crisis (2008-2009), COVID-19 (2019-2023), the Russo-Ukrainian War (2022-) and the many other major events within the 21st century alone? What uncertainties will your organisation or country face?

How then do we understand the future if we cannot predict the future? We can tell stories about the future. Scenarios are vivid mental pictures of the potential but unknowable futures that we create. They:

- Are stories about how the future might unfold and how this might affect an issue that confronts us
- Help us recognise and adapt to changing aspects of our present environment
- Are a method for articulating the different pathways that might exist for us tomorrow and finding our appropriate movements along each of those possible paths.

Scenario planning is a structured way for organisations and countries to think about the future.

Herman Kahn, a defence analyst at RAND Corporation, developed the use of scenario planning after World War II to think about the military and political realities of the days ahead, including nuclear war.

Later in 1961, he founded the Hudson Institute, expanding his focus to include geopolitics, economics, demography, anthropology, education, science and technology, health and urban planning.

Two planners from Shell, Pierre Wack (then Head of Planning at Shell France) and Ted Newland (then Senior Planner at Royal Dutch Shell HQ) sought out Herman Kahn in the 1960s to understand the scenario planning methodology and adapted it to Shell.

In the early 1970s, Pierre Wack and his team built a scenario suggesting that disruptions of the oil supply could result in a sharp rise in prices. The company thus anticipated the crisis that took place in October 1973, when Arab oil-producing countries imposed an oil embargo on Western governments as a consequence of the US support for Israel in the Yom Kippur War. In a few weeks, the price of crude oil increased from $2.50 a barrel to $11, causing a slump in the stock market in Western countries, a contraction of economic activities and a rise in unemployment.

It is useful to note that the scenario process was then not yet formalised, nor was the "oil shock" scenario endorsed by Shell's Committee of Managing Directors (CMD). But Wack and the scenario planners believed in their analysis and, exercising leadership at their level, approached and sensitised managers in various sectors and businesses within Shell. They were successful in securing buy-in from a number of them, though not all. As a result, a large part of Shell was prepared for the shock and Shell was able to act quickly to the market challenges, moving from eighth place in the market to second position. Scenario Planning became endorsed by the CMD and incorporated in Shell's strategic planning. Its value was also recognised beyond Shell. (This was told to me by Shell planners when I was attached to Group Planning from 1991 to 1992.)

The scenarios must be plausible. Plausibility can be strengthened by how relevant and memorable the scenario is, as well as by the logical storyline. If we are writing scenarios for an organisation, they must be relevant to the key decision makers. They must address the key concerns of the top decision makers. The process of scenario planning usually begins with interviewing key decision makers on what they think are the big shifts in society, economics, politics, business and technology that might affect a particular issue; in short, what are their concerns, fears, hopes. You need to know the hidden fears and hopes of the decision makers.

If we are writing scenarios for ourselves, they must be relevant to us. The scenarios must address what is important to us.

Scenarios must be challenging and expand our thinking.

In addition to addressing our concerns (relevance), scenarios examine an array of factors that contribute to the future and fill the gaps in our knowledge and understanding. Scenarios force us to ask, "What if?" and "What would have to be true for the following outcome to emerge?" We learn which drivers matter and which do not – and what will affect those that matter enough to change the scenario.

The scenario building process helps us to identify some particularly powerful drivers of change that result in outcomes that are the inevitable consequence of events that have already happened, or of trends that are already well developed. Shell describes these as "predetermined outcomes". In developing scenarios, organisations should search for predetermined outcomes – particularly unexpected one – and also for key uncertainties and branching points.

Scenarios help us reframe our collective understanding of the present. What Wack called, "The gentle art of re-perceiving the present." In his article "Scenarios: Shooting the Rapids" in *Harvard Business Review* (November 1985), Wack wrote: "Scenarios deal with two worlds; the world of facts and the world of perceptions. They explore for facts, but they aim at perceptions inside the heads of decision makers. Their purpose is to gather and transform information of strategic significance into fresh perceptions."

Mental Map. Perceptions of reality are as relevant for strategic decision-making as reality itself. Every individual has personal and subjective views of the world, of the driving force for change and of cause/effect relationships. Depending on his mental map, an individual will absorb and amplify certain signals, while not noticing or ignoring other signals. Recognition plays a major role: Signals that fit into existing knowledge are more likely to be observed and accepted.

Decisions are based on mental maps. An individual is tempted to consider only options that are compatible with his view of the world. He gives more emphasis to signals and options recognised by his personal models. Any decision he may take therefore tends to be in line with his mental map.

By laying out alternative futures, scenarios allow members of the organisation to challenge conventional wisdom and question the assumptions underpinning today's strategy.

Used effectively, these alternative outlooks can help organisations address difficult issues that need to be explored collaboratively even though there may be deeply divided opinions about them.

From 1991 to 1992, I had the opportunity to spend several months with Royal Dutch Shell Group Planning to work on scenario planning. I learned the methodology as well as interacted with many bright and able team members, including DeAnne Julius (who would later chair the Royal Institute of International Affairs, or more commonly called Chatham House, and also chair the Council of University College London), Adam Kahane, Vince Cable (who would become the UK Secretary of State for Business, Innovation and Skills and also Leader of the Liberal Democrats) and Henry Tan, who was seconded to Group Planning from Shell Singapore. I also met past Shell scenario planners, in particular Kees van der Heijden who invited me to visit the University of Strathclyde where he was then teaching. Besides learning the intricacies of scenario planning from him and enjoying his hospitality, including a visit to a salmon ladder, I also made a presentation on Singapore to his students. Kees had succeeded Peter Schwartz who took over as head of Shell scenario planning from Pierre Wack. Peter and Kees wrote the two best books on scenario planning. Sadly, Kees passed away in 2023. On my return, I worked with a group of very bright civil servants and helped introduce scenario planning to the Singapore Government and the Ministry of Defence.

Scenarios to Strategies to Action

The insights offered by the scenarios are not particularly useful unless we translate them into action.

After we have developed scenarios, how will they be used to help develop a strategic plan? To become fully effective, scenario planning must be embedded in the culture of the organisation. Scenarios must become part of the language used in the organisation for strategic conversation.

The following are some necessary follow-up tasks:

- Quantification of the scenarios to make them useful and ensure internal consistency
- Organising institutional discussion process through meetings, workshops, etc.
- Institutionalising scenarios in the rules of the game of the formal decision-making process

Shell scenarios encompass three different levels of analysis:

1. 'Global scenarios' exploring forces in the global macro-environment encompassing politics, economy, society, ecology, technology and demographics (built every three years and usually covering a time horizon of 20 years)

2. 'Focused scenarios' concerning each business sector of the energy industry and each geographic area in which we operate

3. 'Project scenarios' investigate specific investment projects by processing more detailed information on competitors, profitability, technical and managerial risk

Question about Shell's scenario practice: Did it work?

Did it enable better decisions and therefore create business value?

According to Angela Wilkinson and Roland Kupers ("Living in the Futures", *Harvard Business Review*, May 2013), the answer is:

"YES" in the case of more focused scenarios, and

"Only indirectly" in the case of global scenarios.

There is no evidence that Shell had anticipated the future better than other companies, the way it did in the 1970s oil crisis. Yet Shell continues to bring experts in energy, economics, international affairs and more to create possible visions of the future. I believe this is because there is a realisation that scenario planning helps Shell to be more aware of the external environment – the factors that are beyond the organisation's direct influence – and their changes. Scenario planning explores how this environment might transform the immediate business environment.

What Scenario Planning thinking and practice do is to help leaders navigate the VUCA (volatility, uncertainty, complexity and ambiguity) world and better prepare for futures that might happen.

The organisation can then be faster in catching on to changes in the market and culture.

Can Countries Apply Scenario Planning?

After retiring from Shell in 1982, Wack began consulting for Anglo American, the South African mining corporation, on its efforts to globalise. One of his fascinating insights involved the effect of apartheid on the price of gold production. He said, "South Africans live with the feeling that they are blessed with a geological miracle: their gold and diamond deposits. But it is actually a human miracle: People work in horrible conditions for very low wages. 'Be careful,' I told them. 'You are going to be the highest-cost producer, because this human miracle is not going to last'."

To Anglo American executives, Wack seemed to be predicting the end of apartheid, and they wanted to hear more. So did their spouses; indeed, they wanted to know if there was a future for their children in South Africa, or whether they should emigrate.

An Anglo American executive named Clem Sunter picked up the challenge and, inspired by Wack, suggested two scenarios for the country: a "low road" scenario in which the Whites fought to hold on to apartheid, and a "high road" scenario in which they accepted the inevitability of a multiracial society and pushed for the kind of widespread economic growth that would allow such a society to thrive (in part by bringing South African business back into the flow of the international economy).

Clem Sunter's book, *The World and South Africa in the 1990s* (Cape Town: Tafelberg Publishers, 1987), became a bestseller in South Africa during the late 1980s and early 1990s, second only to Nelson Mandela's autobiography *Long Walk to Freedom*. It is credited with helping

South Africa's White population see the value of a peaceful transition from apartheid (See also Art Kleiner, "The Man Who Saw the Future", *Strategy + Business* Vol. 30 [2003]).

Mont Fleur Scenarios

In 1991, during the South African transition (Nelson Mandela had been released and F. W. de Klerk remained President), Pieter Le Roux was approached to organise a major conference on South Africa's future. He put together a multidisciplinary team of 22 people to work on possible scenarios for South Africa. The team included political office-bearers, academics, trade unionists and business people. It met at Mont Fleur near Stellenbosch in September 1991. Adam Kahane of Shell Scenario Planning acted as facilitator for the exercise. After two further meetings at Mont Fleur (in November 1991 and March 1992) and a lot of work in between, the team reached a consensus on the essential elements of four core scenarios South Africa might follow between 1992 and 2002.

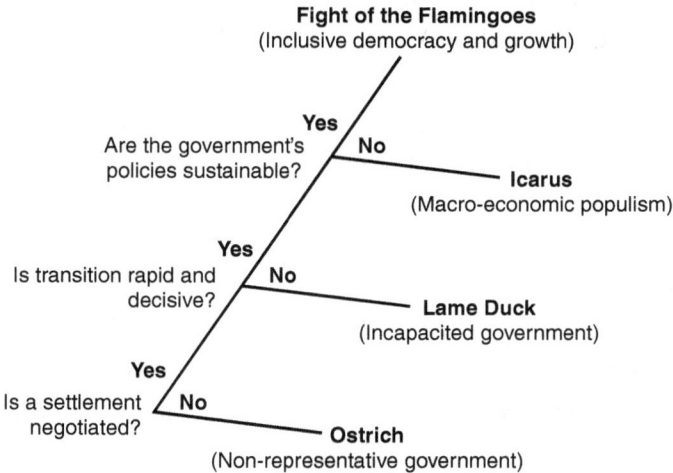

Fight of the Flamingoes
(Inclusive democracy and growth)

Are the government's policies sustainable? **Yes** / **No**

Icarus
(Macro-economic populism)

Is transition rapid and decisive? **Yes** / **No**

Lame Duck
(Incapacited government)

Is a settlement negotiated? **Yes** / **No**

Ostrich
(Non-representative government)

The specific scenarios, while provocative, were not by themselves important. What was important was that the exercise brought together influential people from across diverse organisations to understand the driving forces and to think creatively about the future of their country. The informal network created would help to drive the conversation forward. The Mont Fleur scenarios were published in the South African newspaper *The Weekly Mail & The Guardian Weekly* in July 1992, further facilitating conversation among a larger audience. Adam Kahane wrote that:

> *"Based on my experience in strategic planning, this is one of the most meaningful and exciting scenario planning exercises ever undertaken. The project has shown that a group of experts and leaders with very different perspectives and backgrounds can develop a common understanding of what is going on now in South Africa and might (and should) go into the future. This seems to me to be a very positive sign for the future of the country."*

("The Mont Fleur Scenarios", *Deeper News*, Vol. 30, No. 1)

Can We Apply Scenario Planning for Our Personal Futures?

In my class, I sometimes asked my students to imagine their future. What will they be in 10, 20, 30 years' time in terms of career, family and so on. The exercise sets them thinking about their future, but the problem with a straight-line projection of the present into the future is that the future is unpredictable. How do we prepare for a future that does not turn out the way we have predicted?

I then asked them to do a simple scenario planning exercise:

examine an array of factors that contribute to and determine their possible future. Factors they need to consider include:

- Career: does he remain in the public service or move to the private sector; does he need to upgrade himself, and if so, in which area

- Family: how will his career affect his family life and how will it be impacted by his spousal and family situations

- Health: both his and his immediate family, as well as his ageing parents

- Social: friends, leisure, hobbies

- Purpose: his value to community, contribution to community

- Financial

- Country: is the government and governance good or weak; economic growth and distribution, political stability and law and order; what role can he contribute

- Regional and international matters

In considering their future, students need a deeper insight into the underlying drivers of change. They need to be able to understand what are the pre-determined and what are the key uncertainties and main branching points. How do they prepare themselves for the future? How do they perceive and re-perceive the present?

The usefulness of the scenarios will depend on what questions they ask and how they determine the branching points and choose the axes correctly.

Would the following factors be pre-determined or uncertainties?

- Family – we do not know how things will turn out, especially children. Even spousal relationship should not be taken for granted. But if we realise family is important, it is pre-determined that we will want to invest time to ensure that we do what we can to build a strong family.

- Health – a huge uncertainty – heart, stroke, respiratory, cancer, Alzheimer's, etc. But again, as long as we realise health is important, taking good care of health is a pre-determined – exercise, diet, sleep, mind.
- Social – friends and relationship – is so important. It is pre-determined to nurture it, including cultivating hobbies when young.
- Financial security is so important that financial literacy is a pre-determined.
- Technology in everyday life keeps changing. We do not know what will come next. To stay technologically adept is a pre-determined.
- Career – what is the future of work? How do we keep ourselves relevant?
- Country – what are its future scenarios? What is the future our children will be living in? What role can or should we play?
- International and regional development.

Outcomes in all the above factors may be very uncertain, and it is necessary for us to be aware of the signals and the roles we can play.

When my students did their personal scenarios, a number of them identified family and health as key uncertainties, but others suggested the actions to address them are pre-determined. Some suggested international development (war in Europe, Middle East, Asia) is a key uncertainty, but the events are largely beyond their control. Some suggested career and country. They described the scenarios and then developed strategies on how to improve on their career and their country's future. Some thought more deeply into global issues such as poverty, environment and climate change.

References

Schwartz, Peter. *The Art of the Long View: Planning for the Future in an Uncertain World.* New York: Currency Doubleday, 1991.

Van der Heijden, Kees. *Scenarios: The Art of Strategic Conversation.* NJ: John Wiley & Sons, 2004.

Wack, Pierre. "Scenarios: Shooting the Rapids". *Harvard Business Review,* November 1985.

Wilkinson, Angela & Roland Kupers. "Living in the Futures". *Harvard Business Review,* May 2013.

CHAPTER 6

Courage

Clarity without courage is useless. Courage without clarity is reckless.

What is courage? Courage is:

- mental or moral strength to venture, persevere and withstand danger, fear or difficulty (Merriam-Webster Dictionary)
- the ability to control your fear in a dangerous or difficult situation (Cambridge Dictionary)
- the ability to do something dangerous, or to face pain or opposition, without showing fear (Oxford Dictionary)

Courage is about overcoming our fear, not about fearlessness.

We will still experience fear, but we have the inner strength to overcome our fear and take the necessary action.

There are three main types of Courage:

- Physical – ability to venture in the face of pain, danger, etc.
- Moral – ability to choose to do what is right in the face of opposition, pressure, etc.
- Mental or psychological – ability to proceed in the face of personal doubts, inner fears, etc.

Why is Courage Important in a Leader?

Leaders need courage to make decisions when:

- the situation is difficult
- the problem is complex
- the time is urgent
- the information is incomplete

Leaders need courage to <u>lead change</u> when:

- the people are resistant because they don't understand the need to change and don't feel the sense of urgency
- the solution is untested, and we need to innovate and create new pathways of solving the problem

Leaders need courage to be resilient in the face of adversity (crisis, difficult unexpected problems, war, etc.) to rally people and search for solutions.

Courage leads to clarity. Leaders who are prepared to act and lead decisively create clarity.

At the same time, clarity is needed in order to be courageous. Clarity is important. The first step to being a courageous leader is to have clarity of purpose. A person who has strong clarity in his/her purpose is more likely to overcome fear.

How to Be Courageous?

- Be open to possibilities. Be willing to lean into the unknown to seek answers.

- Embrace risks. Understand that risk-taking and failing are part of life. Take calculated risks, adopt a safe-to-fail rather than fail-safe attitude.
- Display willingness to decide and act.

J.Y. Pillay was the first Chairman of Singapore Airlines (SIA). After being clear about the direction of SIA, he sought a billion dollars to buy a fleet of Boeing 747s. Cabinet approved, and the rest is history. SIA became a great way to fly.

Was it risky? Definitely. But armed with clarity of his team (with Lim Chin Beng as Managing Director), he pushed on.

Too many leaders fail when it comes to the courage test.

As J.Y. Pillay recalled in an interview in 2015:

"We were the only airline in Asia that had the gumption to do these, to think big. Nothing to do with me, I must confess, it all came from management. And we supported them. I could see it, I mean I must say, I had the responsibility of course. Supporting management when they brought these proposals to the board, not rejecting it. When I said no, it would have been no. But I had confidence in management, I knew them well. I saw their record and I noticed that all the carriers around us were so pusillanimous. Most of them were government-owned. No big ambitions. They just wanted a soft life."

Every option has its risks and setbacks. Safe to fail is better than fail safe. Some leaders are afraid of making decisions because they might make the wrong ones, and so they tell their staff they need more data when what they really need is more courage. Courage includes being willing to be vulnerable and to fail. But take calculated risks, not reckless decisions.

Courage is important because it is needed for action. Courage is needed to make critical decisions.

As J.Y. Pillay also said in the same interview:

"The worst thing is to shirk the responsibility of making a decision. Subordinates find that most annoying. Just make a decision; it doesn't matter if it is not the so-called correct decision. If there is a decision we'll all proceed. And if it doesn't lead anywhere, okay, you find some way, you're the leader, you find some way of rectifying it. Incidentally, I don't believe there is any such thing as a perfect decision. There are so many options. Every option has pros and cons, and it's your job as the leader when it comes to the crunch, to decide which you think is the best option. And recognise you may not always be right."

Courage is the conviction to defend your principles and your people. Courage builds trust. A leader's courage empowers others.

Everyday Courage

While courage is important in the people at the top of hierarchy, it is also important in every one of us even when we are not in formal leadership positions.

Putting core principles first, instead of blindly being a "yes-man" to gain approval of superiors and peers, to demonstrate conviction and purpose. Highlight problems. Feedback. Speak up. Be a whistleblower.

How to train and develop courage in our people?

How to build an organisational culture to promote courage?

University of Southern California Professor Kathleen K. Reardon's "Courage as a Skill" (*Harvard Business Review,* January 2007) tells us that in business, courageous action is really "a special kind of calculated risk-taking. People who become good leaders have a greater than average willingness to make bold moves, but they strengthen their chances of success – and avoid career suicide – through careful deliberation and preparation." Business courage is not so much a visionary leader's inborn characteristic as skill acquired through decision-making processes that improve with practice.

Professor Reardon proposes we follow six concrete steps of the "courage calculation" to make success more likely while avoiding rash, unproductive behaviour.

- Setting primary and secondary goals (are your goals personal or organisational? What does success look like in this situation?)
- Determining your goals' importance (if you don't act, will your company suffer?)
- Tipping the power balance in your favour (establish relationships with people in your company)
- Weighing risks and benefits
- Selecting the right time
- Developing contingency plans (what will you do if you don't reach your goals?)

Courage is also needed when we go against groupthink or prevalent sentiments. The 1957 movie *12 Angry Men* has been used in leadership lessons to illustrate this. The movie explores the jury deliberation process in a homicide trial in New York City of a 16-year-old boy accused of murdering his father. The entire movie takes place within the small, hot jury room, intensifying the emotion. Eleven of the jurors, many of whom believe they have heard an iron-clad case against the boy, vote to convict. Only one, Juror #8 played by Henry Fonda, votes "not guilty". He stands against the rest of the jury and is not afraid to voice his commitment to compassion and reason. Arguing that the boy deserves their thoughtful consideration and time, Juror #8 offers to go along with the rest if at the end of discussion, none of the other 11 jurors is prepared to change his mind. This leads to a tense exchange among the 12 jurors, and finally turns around the jury. The movie touches on the power of persuasion, influence, consensus building and, most of all, courage.

A public service leader must have the physical, mental and moral strength to face danger and overcome fear, and the quality of mind or spirit that enables one to face difficulty, danger, pain and any adverse circumstances. Be willing to act on his belief, disagree with and question his boss or go against public sentiment if necessary, of course doing so not in a foolhardy manner.

Courage Can Be Trained

Physical courage is perhaps the easiest to train. Take the example of airborne training for officers in the Singapore Armed Forces. Soon after setting up the Parachute Training Wing in 1974 to train its commandos, the Ministry of Defence decided that it would be good for senior non-commando officers to undergo the basic airborne course which covers static line jumps. Airborne training is probably one of the most stressful activities for soldiers in peacetime. Officers undergoing airborne training will build up their leadership and self-confidence. The Director of General Staff and some of the Colonels and Lieutenant Colonels were among the first to go through the course in 1976. When I returned from my university studies in 1977 as a lieutenant, I received an order to attend the 24/77 basic airborne course. Together with me were two Majors (both were battalion commanders), two Captains, four Lieutenants and a company of young, fearless commando full-time National Servicemen (NSFs). The physical training was tough and the instructors, Commando Sergeants and Warrant Officers, were professional and relentless. Training must be tough as there is a strong correlation between physical fitness and successful airborne training completion. We each completed 10 jumps, including equipment and night jumps, and finished the course with a silver parachute wing pinned on our chests. Discipline, tough training, practice and motivation help to develop confidence and courage.

Manfred F.R. Kets de Vries, a Dutch psychoanalyst, uses the metaphor of muscle as the best way to think of courage. Some people are born with better muscles than others, but everyone can improve their muscles through training and practice. As a psychoanalyst, psychotherapist and executive coach, he advocates the following techniques in helping his patients and students find and practise their courage:

- Create scenarios. By identifying the risks they are taking, people can build immunity to their fears.
- Recognise the negativity bias. By making people aware of the bias (of people attending more to negative than to positive outcomes), they will consider the positive scenarios and also reframe negative scenarios in a more constructive way.
- Talk out the fear beneath. By identifying what people are truly afraid of, we reduce their fear of the situation, which gives them the courage to act.

- Practise going out of your comfort zone. Small acts of courage can have a cumulative effect.

- Manage your body. Fear is physically draining. Take time to eat, exercise and sleep, and keep in physical shape. Relaxation techniques such as meditation and yoga can help create clarity of mind required for courageous action.

- Recognise that you are not alone. Support of people who are in the same boat can help them overcome fear.

We can all learn to develop courage through practice.

Question:

- How do you develop moral courage?

References

Kets de Vries, Manfred F. R. "How to Find and Practice Courage". *Harvard Business Review,* 12 May 2020.

Pillay, Joseph Y. Singapore Civil Service. Interview transcript. Singapore Management University Library Digital Narratives of Asia, 29 June 2015, pp. 1-10.

Reardon, Kathleen K. "Courage as a Skill". *Harvard Business Review,* January 2007.

CHAPTER 7

Communication

Modes of Persuasion

What are good persuasive communications? Aristotle identified three elements.

Of the modes of persuasion furnished by the spoken word there are three kinds.

The first kind depends on the personal character of the speaker [ethos]; the second on putting the audience into a certain frame of mind [pathos]; the third on the proof, or apparent proof, provided by the words of the speech itself [logos].

Persuasion is achieved by the speaker's personal character when the speech is so spoken as to make us think that he is credible.

Ethos – credibility and trust.

Is the person delivering the message credible? Does the audience trust him?

Do they regard him as ethical? Does the person have authority? Is he knowledgeable and competent? Is the person likeable?

Pathos – relates to the emotional appeal – feelings, beliefs, emotions.

Logos – the message must be logical – facts, evidence, statistics, coherent and structured, well-presented.

Ethos, Pathos, Logos – which is most important?

Aristotle seemed to think that logos should be the most important. Aristotle recognised the importance of reasoning when it comes to public speaking, which is why he thought that facts should be the most important part of speaking.

When assessing a policy or programme, we consider logos – the logic and reasoning – to be very important.

But when people choose a leader, they want someone credible and competent whom they trust. Ethos is most important.

When people cannot differentiate (the credibility or competence of the speaker), the ones who appeal to our emotions win. Pathos becomes the most important.

Thus, which is most important is situational. We need to consider all three in successful communications.

Types of Communication

- Written – clear and concise
- Verbal – words, voice
- Non-verbal – body language
- Visual – visual aids, symbols, clothes
- Audio – active listening
- Action – action speaks louder than words

Written communication. The importance of clear and concise written communication is made clear in a speech by Lee Kuan Yew to Ministers of State and senior civil service officers at the Regional Language Centre on 27 February 1979:

"When I was a law student, I learned that every word, every sentence has three possible meanings: what the speaker intends it to mean, what the hearer understands it to mean, and what it is commonly understood to mean. So when a coded message is sent in a telegram, the sender knows what he means, the receiver knows exactly what is meant, the ordinary person reading it can make no sense of it at all.

"When you write notes, minutes or memoranda, do not write in code, so that only those privy to your thoughts can understand. Write so simply so that any other officer who knows nothing of the subject can still understand you. To do this, avoid confusion and give words their ordinary meanings."

In the same speech, he elaborated with the following example:

"Item from the Ministry of Education: (It is necessary to study) the correlation between language aptitude, intelligence and values and attitudes to ensure that the various echelons of leaders are not only effectively bilingual but also of the desirable calibre.

"I read it over and over again. It made no sense. This is gibberish! I inquired and I was told, well, they were trying to find out how language ability and intelligence should influence the methods for instilling good social values and attitudes. Well, then say so. But somebody wanted to impress me by dressing up his ideas in many important words. Next time impress me with the simple way you get your ideas across to me.

"Let me emphasise this point. Before you can put ideas into words, you must have ideas. Otherwise, you are attempting the impossible.

"The written English we want is clean, clear prose. I choose my words carefully – not elegant, not stylish, just clean, clear prose. It means simplifying, polishing and tightening.

"Remember: That which is written without much effort is seldom read with much pleasure. The more the pleasure, you can assume, as a rule of thumb, the greater the effort.

"So when you send me or send your Minister a minute or a memo, or a draft that has to be published like the President's Address, do not try to impress by big words – impress by the clarity of your ideas. Then I am impressed. I speak as a practitioner. If I had not been able to reduce complex ideas into simple words and project them vividly for mass understanding, I would not be here today."

When I joined the Ministry of Finance Revenue Division in 1997, I came across a note on crisp minute writing sent by a previous Permanent Secretary for Revenue Division 20 years earlier in 1977. Mr J.Y. Pillay had written to all Division I and Division II officers then in Revenue Division to remind them of "the need to be precise, brief and performance-oriented in their minute writing". J.Y. Pillay's instruction was that "no sentence should be more than 3 lines long; no paragraph should contain more than 3 sentences". To J.Y. Pillay, minutes could well occupy less than one page and even the most complex subject can be reduced to no more than two pages. My take is that to keep minutes to one to two pages, we must have short, focused decision meetings. There are often too many meetings, and most of these sessions last too long. Of course, brainstorming meetings serve a different purpose. J.Y. Pillay ended the short note with the sentence, "These strictures may appear draconian, but discipline in thinking will make them realisable". Discipline in thinking and communication is indeed important. I believe J.Y. Pillay's instruction should be observed in the spirit, even when it cannot always be adhered in the letter.

<u>Verbal communication.</u> Dwight Eisenhower's D-Day Message to his troops on 6 June 1944 was given to the Forces as it prepared to swarm the Normandy coast. Eisenhower also broadcasted the audio over the radio waves:

"Soldiers, Sailors and Airmen of the Allied Expeditionary Forces:

"You are about to embark upon the Great Crusade, toward which we have striven these many months. The eyes of the world are upon you. The hopes and prayers of liberty-loving people everywhere march with you. In company with our brave Allies and brothers-in-arms on other Fronts you will bring about the destruction of the German war machine, the elimination of Nazi tyranny over oppressed peoples of Europe, and security for ourselves in a free world.

"Your task will not be an easy one. Your enemy is well trained, well equipped and battle-hardened. He will fight savagely. But this is the year 1944. Much has happened since the Nazi triumphs of 1940-41. The United Nations have inflicted upon the Germans great defeats, in open battle, man-to-man. Our air offensive has seriously reduced their strength in the air and their capacity to wage war on the ground.

Our Home Fronts have given us an overwhelming superiority in weapons and munitions of war, and placed at our disposal great reserves of trained fighting men. The tide has turned. The free men of the world are marching together to victory.

"I have full confidence in your courage, devotion to duty, and skill in battle. We will accept nothing less than full victory.

"Good Luck! And let us all beseech the blessing of Almighty God upon this great and noble undertaking."

Eisenhower employed pathos effectively in the short address, delivered to the 175,000-member expeditionary force on the eve of the invasion. He used "you" to indicate that he was speaking directly to the soldiers, sailors and airmen, and "us" in creating the bond between the men and him. He motivated, encouraged, inspired.

How long did he take to write such a short 1.5-minute speech?

Eisenhower started writing the letter in February 1944, and its words were carefully chosen.

What makes a great speech?

Be relevant to your audience.

Ask yourself what problem the audience wants to solve and talk about that problem first. Structure the talk according to "Problem/ Opportunity – Solution – Benefits". Forget fancy PowerPoint presentations and loads of data. Instead, keep your speech simple, with a clear beginning, middle and end. Focus on one theme and eliminate everything else. People don't remember much of what they hear, so focus and keep it simple. Add a few great stories to illustrate if possible. They will remember the stories.

It is not what you say, it is what people hear. The key to successful communication is to take the imaginative leap of putting yourself right into your listener's shoes to know what they are thinking and feeling in the deepest recesses of their mind and heart.

And people can only hear you if you speak up. In a BBC Witness History radio programme broadcasted in October 2017, French feminist Claudine Monteil recalled her first meeting with Simone de Beauvoir in 1970 when she was 21 and Beauvoir, already a very influential writer and feminist activist at 62 years old. Beauvoir had written *The Second Sex*, published in 1949 – the year Monteil was born and was Monteil's idol. Monteil had arrived at Beauvoir's house and sat in front of her, with a group of women waiting to listen to the person she most admired in the world when Beauvoir asked her point blank what was Monteil's point of view and her strategy regarding the abortion campaign. Beauvoir's sister later told Monteil that "you did the right thing, you replied because if you did not reply, you did not exist for her anymore". Beauvoir's father had taught her at an early age not to be afraid to debate and discuss and that was what she expected from everybody. It is important to speak up at a meeting.

<u>Non-verbal communication</u> is important.

The 7-38-55 Rule of Personal Communication (Professor Albert Mehrabian, UCLA, 1967) states that only 7% of communication is by words, while 38% is vocal and 55% is body language.

But Mehrabian's findings of 7-38-55 regarding relative importance of verbal and non-verbal messages that were derived from experiments dealing with communications of feelings and attitudes do not apply for all human communications. For effective and meaningful communication about emotions, these three parts of the message need to support each other – they have to be congruent. In cases of incongruence of verbal and non-verbal communication (of feelings and attitudes), what we say is less important than how we say it.

According to Deborah Gruenfeld, Professor of Leadership and Organizational Behaviour at Stanford University who teaches "The Body Language of Power", "People will decide whether you are competent or not… in less than a hundred millisecond" and so we need to learn to tune our body. Worry less about what we say than how we say it. Learn when to play high (being authoritative, showing up and letting people know that you are in charge) and play low (being approachable, means people feel they can come to you with whatever is on their mind and relate to you on a human level) and how to move between the two effortlessly and consciously.

Listen

Howard Gardner described in his book *Changing Minds: The Art and Science of Changing Our Own and Other People's Minds* an October 2001 meeting between Lawrence Summers, then President of Harvard University, with Cornel West, one of the approximately 15 University Professors then. (The title of University Professor is Harvard's most distinguished professorial post. The position was created in 1935 to honour individuals whose groundbreaking work crosses the boundaries of multiple disciplines, allowing them to pursue research at any of Harvard's Schools. The number of University Professors has increased with new endowed gifts to the university. As of 2024, there are 25.) At the end of the meeting, West was so upset that he considered resigning from the university on the spot. Because he was scheduled for surgery, he decided to postpone his decision until the following spring, when he indeed did resign and went to Princeton University.

Apparently, Summers had been very confrontational, criticising

West for his failure in recent years to carry out serious scholarship and for far-reaching activities off campus.

Summers issued a private apology to West and a public announcement that he is committed to a strong African American Department and to strengthening diversity on campus.

Nevertheless, West left for Princeton. When West had undergone an operation for prostate cancer, Summers did not reach out while Princeton's President and Provost called him regularly during convalescence.

What happened?

Summers' account is that he was new and it was important for him to meet major figures there. He did not know West and had no prejudice. But he had heard some disturbing things about him and wanted to be frank and direct. Summers wanted to see if he could motivate West to do a better job; and that everyone would thank him for this. West's account is that Summers was new to the campus. With no warning, Summers had made accusations against West.

Meetings can go wrong!

Summers and West had gone into the meeting with entirely different mental models of their roles and aspirations.

It is important to create resonance in intimate settings. Gardner's advice for Summers would be:

- First, and importantly, establish common links between the protagonists.

- Second, engage the other (West) in a common enterprise. Suppose Summers wanted West to adopt a tougher stance in grading, he might have asked how he felt the students should be evaluated. Give some scenarios, get responses. If West was not interested, then drop the subject for next time.

- Third, engage in a give and take.

- Fourth, monitor the overall tone of the conversation and keep the atmosphere open, upbeat, optimistic.

- The most important consideration for those engaged in mind change is probably the following: avoid ego-centrism becoming ensnared in one's own construal of events. The purpose of a mind-changing encounter is not to articulate your own point of view but rather to engage the psyche of the other person. In general, the more that one knows of the scripts and the strengths of the other person, the resistances and resonances, and the more that one can engage these fully, the more likely one will be successful in bringing about desired change – or at least holding open the possibility of such changes.

- Another point – how we handle someone who cares about logic, consistency, directness is different from one who is concerned about emotion and respect and non-verbal communications.

Finally, and perhaps the most important form of communication is action. *Action speaks louder than words.*

Communication is particularly important in public service leadership, because leaders have to communicate at different levels and to different groups of citizens with different needs, concerns and biases. Communication must be part of our thinking process and not an afterthought. Certainly it is not to be treated as merely public relations.

Question:

- When do you have to start thinking of communication when you are working on a public policy/programme?

References

Eisenhower, Dwight. *"Order of the Day"*. *Statement as issued to the soldiers, sailors and airmen of the Allied Expeditionary Force on 6 June 1944*. Museum Manuscripts transferred to the Eisenhower Library FY69, Box 1; NAID #12000995.

Gardner, Howard, *Changing Minds: The Art and Science of Changing Our Own and Other People's Minds*, Brighton, MA: Harvard Business Publishing, 2004.

Gruenfeld, Deborah H., "How to Use Body Language for Power", *Lean In*, https://leanin.org/education/power-influence.

CHAPTER 8

Caring-ness

"People don't care how much you know, until they know
how much you care."
Source unknown, but often attributed to
Theodore Roosevelt

How Does a Leader Care?

A caring leader respects his people and treats his people holistically, not as digits for their performance.

He provides psychological and physical space for people to build connections with one another, and share trust and respect.

He cares for his people's health – both physical and mental.

He provides an environment that ensures fairness and justice.

People trust their leaders to have their best interest at heart.

A caring leader gives voice and consideration to his people.

Listening – listens to their views, perspectives and problems, and receives feedback, suggestions as well as criticisms.

Engaging and empowering – involves his people, empowering them.

People must feel they are involved, that they contribute and take ownership.

A caring leader believes in his people – enables them, challenges them to do their best, covers their backs. People can become the best they can be under such leadership.

A caring leader ensures his people grow – in capability, effectiveness, wisdom, resilience, etc. He must have a growth-oriented mindset towards his team and people, not just facilitate their work and recognition. This is especially since a person spends at least one-third of his life at the workplace.

A caring leader serves the needs of his people.

Robert Greenleaf, widely credited as the founder of the modern "Servant Leadership" movement, believes the betterment of others to be the true intention of a servant leader.

But the philosophy of servant leadership is not new. Greenleaf credits his reading of Hermann Hesse's 1932 novella, *Journey to the East*, as the personal source of inspiration in his coining the term "servant-leader" in his 1970 essay "The Servant as Leader".

Journey to the East details a group of philosophers, writers, musicians and artists travelling through time and space in search of the ultimate truth during the aftermath of the Great War. One day, the humble servant Leo disappears, leading to confusion because unknowing to the members, it was Leo who has held the group together. Distress and dissension break out among the members, and the party eventually disintegrates. Years later, Leo was revealed as the President of the League.

Servant Leadership

Servant Leadership Philosophy is important as it reminds us to:

- Serve others' needs
- Focus on leaders meeting the needs of others
- Focus on people (not on process)
- Be people driven; person-oriented

Leaders' values should, among others, include:

- Listening
- Humility
- Integrity
- Empathy
- Appreciation of others
- Communication

In short, leaders must be caring.

Why it is important to remember that "To Lead is to Serve"?

Some individuals who reach leadership positions may feel that they have earned it because they have undergone years of training and trials, service and sacrifice. Or that they have superior intellect and capability, that they are the best people, most capable and most qualified, to lead the organisation and that they deserve recognition and huge rewards. They begin to feel entitled and forget to serve.

Entitled leaders become arrogant – believing their way to be the best way, that they deserve special treatment and privileges – are easily offended and want to be served rather than to serve.

In an opinion piece titled "Sex, Lies and Magical Thinking About CEO Behaviour" in the *Financial Times* on 16 September 2023, FT columnist Brooke Masters writes:

> *"Perhaps the nature of a chief executive's job makes some occupants vulnerable to magical thinking, both about what they are entitled to do and what they can get away with. Deeply driven and surrounded by those who defer to their judgment, it is easy to start to believe that ordinary rules do not apply."*

"Good decision making is a social activity, yet the system defies CEOs and is designed to suppress dissent," said Roger Steare, a corporate philosopher. He argues that boards need to spend more time looking at the moral character of the people they promote and testing how potential CEOs react to personal pressure.

(Masters was writing about the BP chief executive who quit early in the week after admitting he had failed to fully disclose his past relationships with his work colleagues.)

The philosophy of a servant leadership is especially important for public servants and public service leaders. As the name denotes, a public servant is a servant to the public.

However, servant leadership does not mean the leader is captured by the public or lets the public dictate what to do. There are two components to servant leadership:

- <u>Leadership aspect</u> – when we set the vision and the direction according to what is right for the country and lead the people.

- <u>Servant aspect</u> – when we design a policy or programme, we are focused on how best to serve the people, not what we think our boss or the organisation would like.

A caring leader ensures that the organisation is led by able leaders at all levels.

People must trust that their leaders are capable and reliable, can deliver successful outcomes, and can motivate and build resilience to face hardships.

(It is demotivating to work under an undeserving leader.)

This means meritocracy. No favouritism, cronyism or nepotism. People move up only if they perform. Everyone with skill and imagination may aspire to reach the highest level.

The system must be open, transparent and fair. What constitutes as merit is widely accepted, and not based on some heuristics.

Good work must be rewarded and recognised. Work for reward and reward for work.

What constitutes good work? Who contributes to the success? We must appreciate that a successful outcome is often the work of many people in the team over a period of time. We must also remember those who worked before us, the shoulders upon whom we sit. And the role that luck plays.

A caring leader respects his people by:

- treating every person with dignity
- assigning each person to a job according to his/her ability
- providing opportunities for the individual to improve and develop his talents, taking into consideration individual and organisational needs
- recognising each person's contribution to the team's success

Pay differential is necessary but should not be extreme.
Reward must be externally competitive and internally equitable.

However, recognising that every team needs all its members to perform and diverse skills are required – some skills which are highly sought after need higher rewards. Differential in reward is necessary but how large should it be in order to be useful and desirable? Watch out for extreme pay differentials which can become dysfunctional.

How do we recognise each person's role in an organisation? What is the proper wage ratio?

From its start, Ben & Jerry's (ice cream) established that from top to bottom, the ratio should not be greater than 5:1. When Ben Cohen was set to retire in 1994 and no successor could be found, the ratio was raised to 7:1 to attract new talents. Over a number of years, it was raised to 17:1. When it was acquired by Unilever USA in 2000, the ratio was removed.

Fast Company (18 July 2022) cited an AFL-CIO (American Federation of Labor and Congress of Industrial Organizations) study Executive Paywatch Report which reveals that S&P 500 CEOs averaged $18.3 million in compensation for 2021 – *324 times* the median worker's pay, and higher than both 2020's pay ratio (299:1) and 2019's ratio (264:1). (Note: This is top to medium, not top to bottom as in Ben & Jerry's). "Instead of investing in their workforce by raising wages and keeping the prices of their goods and services in check, their solution was to reap record profits from rising prices and cause a recession that would put working people out of our jobs," said Fred Redmond, AFL-CIO's secretary-treasurer in his 18 July 2022 speech "Runaway CEO Pay Has Created a Perfect Storm for 'Greedflation'".

The average total compensation for S&P 500 CEOs saw a $2.8 million (or 18.2%) increase from 2020. Inflation for 2021 was 7.1%, and workers' wages rose just 4.7% for the year. Workers' real wages fell 2.4% in 2021, after adjusting for inflation.

The same magazine also reported that McDonald's CEO Chris Kempczinski earned 2,251 times more than the average worker; Starbucks' ex-CEO, Kevin Johnson, took home 1,579 times more.

Does money motivate? Ray Fitzgerald, a popular sports commentator, wrote in the *Boston Globe*, 5 January 1978 a story about a conversation between an owner of a sports team and his general manager (GM).

"Explain to me about motivation," said the owner. The GM said, "The coach has to make his players feel wanted. He has to make them feel they're contributing. He has to make them feel good."

The owner thought that over. "The last time I looked at my books, I was paying about two and a half million dollars a season in salaries. Doesn't that make them feel wanted? Doesn't that make them feel good?"

"It would be," said the GM. "But times have changed. All that money simply makes our players self-satisfied. Big cash ties their legs together so they can't dive for loose balls and turn their brains into fettuccini, so they can't figure out when to switch and when to play their own man."

A leader must be competent, able to enlarge the pie. He must be well remunerated. But how much is enough? How best to divide the pie such that it is considered fair?

The leader should be both loved and feared, not just loved or feared.

The leader must have the ability to inspire and motivate people, rally them around. Do what is right, not what is popular. People are willing to follow him because they trust him; they both love and fear him.

To quote Niccolò Machiavelli in *The Prince*:

"Upon this a question arises: whether it be better to be loved than feared or feared than loved? One should wish to be both, but, because

it is difficult to unite them in one person, it is much safer to be feared than loved."

Why do some leaders lack caring-ness? Caring-ness takes effort. The leader must be competent and confident. He must be able to allocate his time and not be overloaded with urgent work.

The caring leader must avoid being over-caring. Just like the overprotective parent who wants to protect his children from pain, from hurt, from disappointment and from failure, which will result in the child being scared and not develop, there are adverse effects to being over-caring.

How to spot when you are an over-caring leader?

When you avoid making difficult decisions because you are concerned about the staff's reaction.

When you micro-manage or try to pre-empt failure.

When you shy away from holding difficult conversations with the staff.

The act of caring when taken too far can be a control issue. There is also need to avoid staff taking advantage. Caring does not mean being indecisive. Be caring and be firm.

Questions:

- ◆ How does a leader care?
- ◆ Can there be too much caring?

CHAPTER 9

Culture

"Culture eats strategy for breakfast."
Peter Drucker

This may be Drucker's most enduring mis-quotation. It's catchy and it echoes his caution to managers about culture's durability. According to the Drucker Institute, what Peter Drucker did say is: "Culture – no matter how defined – is singularly persistent".

What is Culture?

Why is it important? And what is the leader's role?

According to Edgar Schein, MIT professor and expert in organisational culture:

- Culture is what a group learns over a period of time as that group solves its problems of survival in an external environment and its problems of internal integration.

- Three fundamental levels at which culture manifests itself are:
  - observable artifacts
  - values
  - basic underlying assumptions

- When one enters an organisation, one observes and feels its *artefacts*.

- Deeply held assumptions often start out historically as values but, as they stand the test of time, gradually come to be taken for granted and then take on the character of assumptions. They are no longer questioned and they become less and less open to discussion.

What Roles Do Leaders Play?

When groups or organisations first form, there are usually dominant figures or "founders" whose own beliefs, values and assumptions provide a visible and articulated model for how the group should be structured and how it should function. As these beliefs are put into practice, some work out and some do not. The group then learns from its own experience what parts of the "founder's" belief system work for the group as a whole. The joint learning then gradually creates shared assumptions.

Schein explains that culture is dynamic – it can evolve with new experiences, leaders and changing environment.

Cultural Dynamics can occur in one of the following ways:

- Natural Evolution – there is constant pressure (changing environment, new members with new beliefs) on any given culture to evolve and grow

- Guided Evolution – enhanced cultural elements that are viewed as critical to maintaining identity and to promote the "unlearning" of cultural elements that are viewed as increasingly dysfunctional

- Managed Change – leaders of organisations sometimes are able to overcome their own cultural biases and perceive that elements of an organisation's culture are dysfunctional for survival and growth in a changing environment

Schein further stressed that understanding an organisation's culture is important. It is especially important for a manager to understand the culture in a detailed way when:

1. he or she joins a new organisation as a manager;
2. one company acquires another (or when a new boss comes in);
3. the manager is coordinating the efforts of different functional groups within his or her organisation; and
4. the manager is confronting the need to fundamentally change the company's strategic direction and, by implication, its culture.

When Bill Bratton joined NYPD as the Police Commissioner, one of the first things he did was to arrange for a culture diagnostic of the department and to understand the police officers. This is important. A new leader should not simply decide on what he wants done without understanding the culture of the department. Only by understanding the culture can he influence and motivate the men to attain the goals he wants. Similarly, when I first went to the Urban Redevelopment Authority as its CEO, I had an exercise conducted to understand the culture and then worked with the staff to improve it.

An understanding of the whys and wherefores of an organisation's culture is important, as can be illustrated by the five monkeys experiment.

The experiment is used to illustrate that people often follow established behaviour in the workplace. Instead of challenging entrenched assumptions, many of us, like the monkeys, simply keep reproducing what has been done before. It is the easiest thing to do.

The Experiment

A group of scientists placed 5 monkeys in a cage and in the middle, a ladder with bananas on top.

Every time a monkey went up the ladder, the scientists soaked the rest of the monkeys with cold water.

After a while, every time a monkey went up the ladder, the other ones beat up the one on the ladder.

After some time, no monkey dare to go up the ladder regardless of the temptation.

Scientists then decided to substitute one of the monkeys. The first thing this new monkey did was to go up the ladder. Immediately the other monkeys beat him up.

After several beatings, the new member learned not to climb the ladder even though never knew why.

The second monkey was substituted and the same occurred. The first monkey participated on the beating for the second monkey. A third monkey was changed and the same was repeated. The fourth was substituted and the beating was repeated and finally the fifth monkey was replaced.

What was left was a group of 5 monkeys that even though never received a cold shower, continued to beat up any monkey who attempted to climb the ladder.

If it was possible to ask the monkeys why they would beat up all those who attempted to go up the ladder, their answer would be: "I don't know. That's how things are done around here."

Don't miss the opportunity to share this with others as they might be asking themselves why we continue to do what we are doing if there is a different way out there.

Conclusion:
Don't follow others behavior, think before you follow.

Except there was no such experiment. Some writers attribute the story to an experiment by Gordon R. Stephenson in 1967. He did conduct an experiment with monkeys, but there were no bananas, no stairs, nor spraying with cold water mentioned in the study. His experiment, "Cultural Acquisition of a Specific Learned Response among Rhesus Monkeys", with some different parameters, shows that the newcomer will most likely teach the others to no longer fear the old. There is also a gender issue: Female monkeys learn by observation, male by "punishment".

Over the years, there have been so many versions that it is unclear who created the fictionalised versions of the Stephenson experiment. As long as we treat the story as an anecdote and not a scientific experiment, we can learn powerful lessons from it.

Socialisation

Culture perpetuates and reproduces itself through the socialisation of new members entering the group. The socialisation process really begins with recruitment. Selection in that the organisation is likely to look for new members who already have the "right" set of assumptions, beliefs and values. They also need to be trained and "acculturated". Culture is also shaped through rewards and recognition.

Culture is vital to sustaining organisational and societal values.

I use two cases to teach organisational culture. One is the Boeing 737 Max crash and the other the Deepwater Horizon oil spill. Both illustrated how Boeing and BP lost their engineering excellence and safety culture, respectively. More importantly for public service leaders, they also illustrated how the regulators, Federal Aviation Administration and Mineral Management Service respectively, have lost their competence to regulate and serve the public. A short note on the two cases is in Chapter 9.1.

Questions:

◆ What is the culture of your organisation?

◆ How can you change the culture?

References

Christensen, Clayton. "What is an Organization's Culture?" *Harvard Business Review*, February 1999.

Stephenson, G. R. "Cultural Acquisition of a Specific Learned Response Among Rhesus Monkeys". In *Progress in Primatology*, edited by D, Starek, R. Schneider & and H.J. Kuhn. Stuttgart: Fischer, 1967.

Case Studies on Culture
Boeing 737 Max and
Deepwater Horizon Oil Spill

L et us look at two cases to discuss the importance of culture – a Harvard Business School case study on Boeing 737 Max ("What Went Wrong with Boeing's 737 Max?" HBS 9-320-104) and a Harvard Kennedy School case study on "The Deepwater Horizon Oil Spill: The Politics of Crisis Response" (A) (HKS Case 1981.0.3).

Boeing Culture

On 29 October 2018, Lion Air Flight 610 crashed in Indonesia, killing 189. On 9 March 2019, Ethiopian Airlines Flight 302 crashed killing 157. Both incidents involved a Boeing 737 Max aircraft.

Boeing is an American icon, revered throughout the world for its engineering innovation. It was founded in 1911 by William Boeing as an engineering-first enterprise. Boeing is clear that the way it operates starts with engineering excellence: "A strong engineering foundation enables us to build and maintain our products with safety, quality and integrity in the factory and in service. Our customers expect it. That's why we will always take the time to get the engineering right."

What happened? "The safety culture has been corrupted under

pressure from Wall Street, and executives and board members who were looking more at their bonuses than at the integrity of their organisation," commented US Representative Peter DeFazio, chair of the US House Committee on Transportation and Infrastructure. In 1997, Boeing acquired McDonnell Douglas. Corporate culture started moving "away from expensive, ground-breaking engineering towards a more cut-throat culture devoted to keeping costs down". Leadership's focus also shifted. Share repurchases outpaced research and development spending. In 2001, Boeing shifted its HQ from Seattle to Chicago. Its CEO was quoted as saying, "We believe having a HQ separate from any of our businesses will help us grow."

Under external competition from Airbus, in particular A320neo, Boeing rushed to modify its successful 737 aircraft. It went for amended type certification (which takes three to five years for the Federal Aviation Administration [FAA] to approve) instead of new aircraft type certification (five to nine years). It did not explain the Manoeuvring Characteristics Augmentation System (MCAS), a new flight stabilising feature, to the regulator (FAA), nor to the pilots (to obviate the need for pilots to have simulator training on the new aircraft and thus save the airline companies time and resources).

After the two crashes, on 11 March 2019, China ordered a dozen carriers to ground their 96 planes – about a quarter of all 737 Max aircraft in operation globally. Authorities in Ethiopia, Indonesia, Mongolia, Morocco and Singapore quickly followed suit, along with carriers in Latin America and South Korea. Despite the FAA issuing a statement backing the Boeing jet's airworthiness, the European Union grounded the model, as did at least 10 other countries, with authorities saying the aircraft would not be allowed to fly to or from their countries pending the investigation. On 4 April 2019, Boeing publicly acknowledged that MCAS played a role in both accidents.

FAA Culture

What about the culture in the Federal Aviation Administration?

Safety is at the core of FAA's mission. But because of inadequate manpower and resources, FAA relied on engineers at Boeing to provide technical expertise and insight. In 2009, FAA created the Boeing Aviation Safety Oversight Office dedicated to overseeing of Boeing and staffed primarily by Boeing personnel. It granted amended certification for 737 Max in 2017 (Boeing had applied for amended type certification in 2012).

The most significant findings of the US Senate Committee Investigation Report Dec 2020 on Aviation Safety Oversight included the following:

- FAA senior managers had not been held accountable for failure to develop and deliver adequate training in flight standards despite repeated findings of deficiencies over several decades.

- The FAA continued to retaliate against whistleblowers instead of welcoming their disclosures in the interest of safety.

- The FAA repeatedly permitted Southwest Airlines to continue operating dozens of aircraft in an unknown airworthiness condition for several years. These flights put millions of passengers at potential risk.

- During the 737 Max recertification testing, Boeing inappropriately influenced FAA human factor simulator testing of pilot reaction times involving an MCAS failure.

- FAA senior leaders may have obstructed a Department of Transportation Office of Inspector General (DOT OIG) review of the 737 Max crashes.

Culture is Sticky

Boeing fired its CEO, Dennis Muilenburg, in 2019 following the two 737 Max crashes. Has the safety culture improved?

On 5 January 2024, a door plug (a structure installed to replace an optional emergency exit door) on an Alaska Airlines Boeing 737 Max aircraft, which was not bolted in place due to a manufacturing error, blew out causing an uncontrolled decompression of the aircraft. The aircraft, which had taken off from Portland, returned to Portland for an emergency landing. All 171 passengers and six crew members survived the accident, with three receiving minor injuries. A preliminary report of the National Transportation Safety Board (NTSB) published on 6 February said that four bolts, intended to secure the door plug, had been missing when the accident occurred and that Boeing records showed evidence that the plug had been reinstalled with no bolts prior to initial delivery of the aircraft.

DeFazio shared the following post on LinkedIn:

"Two days ago Boeing fired the head of the 737 Max line. Yet another fall guy in the totally dysfunctional corporate culture at Boeing. The current CEO Calhoun served on the Board during the whole Max development disaster – but he says he knew nothing about the rushed production and concealment of MCAS to drive stock price. His expertise in aerospace design, engineering and production is nil. He has a bachelors in accounting and his resume touts his time with Blackstone – a private equity group who prides themselves on extracting value – i.e. gutting companies for a big payout and then cashing in. He continued to push for a frenzied pace of production for the 737 until the Portland door plug blow out. He and other senior management and Board Members who have no expertise nor

interest in safe competent design and production of aircraft need to go if Boeing is to recover its reputation and role as the greatest aerospace manufacturer in the world. But hey he might make more money breaking up the company and selling the fragments – that's what Blackstone would do."

Culture is indeed sticky.

Deepwater Horizon Oil Spill

The Deepwater Horizon oil spill, the largest marine oil spill, was caused by an explosion on the Deepwater Horizon oil rig in the Gulf of Mexico and its subsequent sinking on 22 April 2010. The oil rig was operated by offshore-oil-drilling company Transocean, and leased by oil company BP. The explosion was caused by the natural gas blasting through the concrete core installed by Halliburton to seal the well for later use.

BP Safety Culture

BP has proclaimed the importance of safety for its vast worldwide operations. "Our goal of 'no accidents, no harm to people and no damage to the environment' is fundamental to BP's activities," stated the company's Sustainability Review 2009. "We work to achieve this through consistent management processes, ongoing training programmes, rigorous risk management and a culture of continuous improvement." It added that "creating a safe and healthy working environment is essential for our success. Since 1999, injury rates and spills have reduced by approximately 75%." Yet despite the improvement in injury and spill rates during that decade, BP has caused a number of disastrous or potentially disastrous workplace incidents that suggest its approach to managing safety has been on individual worker occupational safety but not on process safety. These incidents and subsequent analyses indicate that the company does not have consistent and reliable risk-management processes – and thus has been unable to meet its professed commitment to safety. BP's safety lapses have been chronic.

BP, Halliburton, Transocean: Who is Responsible?

BP blamed Transocean for the slick, since it was in charge of safety in the drilling operations. Transocean said that it had leased the rig to BP, which held the concession for the site. Also it had subcontracted to Halliburton the task of building the casing around the well and its valves. Halliburton laid the responsibility on BP and Transocean.

BP, as the responsible party that caused the spill, is clearly legally and professionally responsible for containing the spill and mitigating its harmful consequences. BP holds the oil lease or concession. But Deepwater Horizon oil rig is owned and operated by offshore oil drilling company Transocean (the world's largest offshore drilling contractor). The leaks (surge) were from the concrete core installed by contractor Halliburton in order to seal the well for later use.

Responsibility Cannot Be Delegated

In September 2014, US District Judge Carl Barbier said that BP was mostly to blame for the Deepwater Horizon oil spill, which killed 11 people and spewed oil into the water for 87 days. Barbier attributed 67% of the fault to BP; 30% to Transocean, which owned the Deepwater Horizon drilling rig; and 3% to Halliburton, the cement contractor.

Basically, responsibility cannot be delegated.

Minerals Management Service

A bigger problem is with the government regulation. The Minerals Management Service (created in 1982 under the Secretary of the Interior) oversaw both offshore leasing and enforcement. It was generating revenue from offshore drilling while simultaneously regulating the industry, creating possible conflict of interest. Oversight had taken a back seat to leasing. MMS had fewer than 60 inspectors to cover over 3,000 offshore facilities and had never established an environmental enforcement programme. Regulators had not kept pace with the offshore industry, which was increasingly outsourcing work to contractors while drilling deeper and deeper.

MMS exempted BP from various safety requirements. It approved BP's exploration plan in less than a month of review, exempting it from detailed analysis. "BP said in its oil exploration plan there'd be no significant impact on any natural resources. And MMS went along."

Lack of Expert Knowledge

MMS had basically no expertise in the area. It relied on expertise from the American Petroleum Institute (API, "a lobbying powerhouse representing more than 650 corporate members").

MMS never achieved the reform of its regulatory oversight of drilling safety consonant with practices that most other countries had embraced decades earlier.

The API asked to be allowed to develop an offshore safety standard. The agency urged companies to adopt safety and environmental management systems voluntarily, and hinted that wide industry participation might prevent a formal rulemaking. By this time, there appeared to have been a working assumption within both the agency and the industry it was charged with overseeing that technological advances had made equipment remarkably reliable.

MMS' approach is "We want to approach our relationship with the offshore industry more as a partner than a policeman. We need to create an atmosphere where the primary concern is to fix the problem, not the blame."

MMS Culture and Leadership

The National Commission on the BP Deepwater Horizon Oil Spill and Offshore Drilling, formed by the US President in May 2010, faulted the administration's response to the spill in a report issued in October.

On agency leadership and technical expertise, the Commission found that "no one who has led MMS since it was created almost 30 years ago has possessed significant training or experience in petroleum engineering or petroleum geology, or any significant technical expertise related to drilling safety. In the absence of a clear statement from the top about the necessity for such expertise to ensure drilling safety, it should be no surprise that MMS personnel have suffered from the loss of essential expertise throughout their ranks. Indeed, the lack of requisite training is abysmal".

Revenue generation – enjoyed both by industry and government – became the dominant objective. But there was a hidden price to be paid for those increased revenues. Any revenue increases dependent on moving drilling further offshore and into much deeper waters came with a corresponding increase in the safety and environmental risks of such drilling. Those increased risks, however, were not matched by greater, more sophisticated regulatory oversight. Industry regularly and intensely resisted such oversight, and neither Congress nor any of a series of presidential administrations mustered the political support necessary to overcome that opposition.

In the end, the blame should not be on just the companies and the regulator. The political leadership and the public were also to blame. Insatiable consumption of oil by the public and the economy pushed the US Government towards deeper offshore drilling. Drilling in deep-water brings new risks, not yet completely addressed by the reviews of where it is safe to drill, what could go wrong and how to respond if something does go awry. Neither industry nor government adequately addressed these risks. Investments in safety, containment and response equipment and practices failed to keep pace with the rapid move into deep-water drilling. Absent major crises, and given the remarkable financial returns available from deep-water reserves, the business culture succumbed to a false sense of security.

Crises expose dysfunctional organisational cultures.

Beyond an Organisation's Culture

To fully understand the meaning of different observed behaviours and espoused values, one must understand the underlying paradigm that the members of the organisation use to structure their reality.

Edgar Schein did a study on Singapore's Economic Development Board (EDB) and wrote in *Strategic Pragmatism: The Culture of Singapore's Economics Development Board* (1996) that in the EDB, two different paradigms were operating. One paradigm consists primarily of a set of assumptions that Singapore's leaders held about economic development. These assumptions are shared by the EDB, and they also provide a broader context within which the EDB operates. The other paradigm consists of a set of assumptions about how the EDB structures and manages itself.

The two paradigms together must be viewed as a total system rather than as individual elements. What makes EDB work is the simultaneous and coordinated effect of all of the different shared tacit assumptions.

The contextual paradigm comprises assumptions about the role of government in economic development. The cultural paradigm of the organisation comprises assumptions about the organisation and management in the EDB. The effectiveness of the EDB depends on not itself alone, but the role of the Singapore Government which he lists, among others:

- State capitalism – government involvement in private enterprise
- Absolute long-range political stability
- Collaboration among sectors
- An incorruptible, competent civil service: clear rules and kept promises
- Primacy of people and meritocracy
- Strategic pragmatism (the strategic glue that ties the paradigm together)

References

"What Went Wrong with Boeing's 737 Max?" *Harvard Business School*, 9-320-104.

"The Deepwater Horizon Oil Spill: The Politics of Crisis Response" (A) (Harvard Kennedy School Case 1981.0.3) (2013).

CHAPTER 10

Linking up the 5Cs into a Framework

includes Bao Yilun's essay, "Shaping Leadership Heartware with 5Cs"

In discussing the 5Cs, I began with Clarity, then Courage, Communication, Caring-ness and Culture. It is a useful and logical sequence. However, which of the 5Cs to start with would depend on the circumstances. In some situations, courage may be the starting point. The government needs to carry out necessary but unpopular policies and courage is needed. In other situations, communications may be the starting point as winning the hearts and minds of the people is key. Yet, because the public service serves the public, care for the people and what they need is the starting point.

It is not necessary to follow the 5Cs in any sequence. Nor is the relationship linear. What is important is to consider all 5Cs with regard to how we carry out our public service leadership.

After my lectures, I gave my students an assignment to write about the "5Cs of Leadership Framework. What do I understand by the 5Cs? Comment, critique and improve on them. How have and/or will I apply the 5Cs of Leadership in my work and life?". Their essays reflect very good understanding of the concepts and I have also learned much from them.

One of my MPA (Academic Year 2023-24) students, Bao Yilun, a civil servant in the Foreign Affairs Office of the Shanghai Government, serving as programme officer and English/French interpreter for city leadership, has written an essay entitled "Shaping Leadership Heartware with 5Cs", linking up the 5Cs into a framework as follows:

- Clarity to Guide Hearts
- Courage to Strengthen Hearts
- Communication to Motivate Hearts
- Caring-ness to Warm Hearts
- Culture to Transform Hearts

I find the essay offers an interesting and refreshing perspective and include it here with her permission.

Shaping Leadership Heartware with 5Cs

Bao Yilun

Hardware to Heartware

Two major kinds of power exist for leadership, position power and personal power (Northouse, 2013). Along these lines, we can distinguish between transactional leadership and transformational leadership. This is pertinently illustrated in the example of Henry Ford who allegedly said, "Why is it that every time I want to hire a pair of hands, I get a brain attached?" Transactional leadership, driven by positional power or authority, KPIs and rewards/penalties (hardware), reduces employees to mere pairs of hands. However, in a transformational leadership mindset underpinned by personal power, which values and empowers individual needs and growth (heartware), these words could be flipped into "With every pair of hands, you get a free brain." (Bessant, 2015). A transformational leader inspires whereas a transactional leader orders. As countries move into knowledge economies, a people-centric leadership style that leverages heartware gains prominence. This is where the 5Cs framework comes in helpful for leaders to draw more strength from personal power rather than positional power, and to shift from hardware to heartware to drive meaningful transformations.

Clarity to Guide Hearts

Clarity in mindset, purpose and direction is of utmost importance in the 5Cs, as a leader's vision will influence followers' behaviours (Strange, 2022). A true transformational leader should have a clear and compelling vision other than KPIs to garner support.

This might seem to be straightforward but there are two major pitfalls that leaders should be wary of. First, clearly define the problem facing your organisation. How a problem is defined will shape what is done about it (Stone, 1989). When a leader is unable to critically dissect the complexity of issues, or confuses symptoms with causes, he will just be beating around the bush or worse, going in the wrong direction; this will spell disaster for his organisation. Secondly, know your bias. As the leader engages in a sense-making process to understand the root challenges, two processes are solicited, namely technical processes, whereby the leader relies on scenario-planning and cost-benefit analysis to create a technical understanding of the potential risks, as well as the reflexive process, which is based on his own expertise, experience and judgment. The latter is more critical since at the end of the day, it's the leader who decides. However, leaders could fall prey to heuristics and cognitive biases in the process. For example, in some public organisations in China, some leaders are subject to red tape, inertia and conflicting goals across departments, and they tend to be strongly biased towards the status quo, and prefer proposals with incremental changes when fundamental changes are really needed. I for example would be mindful to reconfigure and expand my consultation circle to seek clarity. Conducting informal consultations with ordinary rank and file and fringe staff could also help expand my horizons for additional insights and to gain clarity in judgment.

Courage to Strengthen Hearts

Courage is indispensable in making things happen. While leaders recognise it is the only way to power through with real progress, there are three pitfalls to look out for.

First, courage is dangerous without clarity. When engaging in risk-taking, leaders should be rigorous in recognising the unknown, predicting risks and calculating payoffs – achieving strong clarity. Second, moral courage is not something you are born with – it must be cultivated and developed (Novogratz and McNulty, 2022). I'm not a Type T person, but I'm heartened to learn that qualities related to courage such as self-efficacy and openness to new experiences can be nurtured through mindful learning and training. Thirdly, a fearless organisation (Edmondson, 2018) works better than a single fearless leader. Building systems of trust and psychological safety to foster courageous employees who can admit mistakes, trial new ideas or simply dare to ask a stupid question could drive overall innovation and loyalty. What

I will do is establish a regular practice of open and honest discussions with team members during project reviews and recognise and reward their candour and new ideas.

Communication to Motivate Hearts

Even if you have clarity in vision and the courage to act, the ability to inspire and motivate through effective communication of your vision is essential in implementation.

I observe three ways through which leaders can enhance communication.

First, know your audience. The characteristics and the latitudes of acceptance of your audience determine your modes of persuasion. For example, when the audience is academics, you can go with Logos – logic, and reasoning. If the audience is grassroot workers, Pathos – emotions and beliefs might resonate better. If the audience is simply tired of being fooled for so long and is looking for a new credible leader they can trust, you appeal to Ethos – authority and trustworthiness, endorsed by competence, accomplishments or past track record.

Secondly, highlight the shared values that best resonate with the audience, so that they can identify with something larger than themselves and be connected to a larger community (Shamir, House, Arthur, 1993). People will find their work worthwhile and fulfilling when they feel like they are pursuing a higher purpose.

Thirdly, congruence in communication. As many leaders I observe often carefully choose uplifting and inclusive words to use in their verbal communication, they often neglect non-verbal communication which might just give them away. Effective leadership requires being highly congruent in both verbal and nonverbal spheres of communication. Furthermore, social psychologist Amy Cuddy stresses that leaders themselves are influenced by their own non-verbal behaviours. This I deem is especially true for female leaders. Women, like myself, are by nature less predisposed when it comes to projecting authoritative body language. We should learn to harness non-verbal strategies to assert authority and meanwhile build up our own confidence to navigate challenging patriarchal work settings.

Caringness to Warm Hearts

As important as a message may be, it cannot get across without caringness. The key enabler for the other heartwares is thus caringness, meaning to develop and empower people based on respect and empathy.

However, caringness is more important in some cultures than others. One study (Gentry, 2016) I found interesting shows that caringness is more critical to leadership performance in high power-distance[1] society (China, Singapore, etc.) where people give great deference to a person of authority. This holds particular relevance in organisations where strict hierarchy characterises leader-subordinate relationships, personal and professional

---

[1] Power distance is defined as "the degree to which members of an organization or society expect and agree that power should be stratified and concentrated at higher levels of an organization or government" (House & Javidan, 2004, p. 12).

support provided to staff as a caring parent could go a long way in warming the hearts and minds, creating cohesion and loyalty, and thus unlocking potential and productivity.

Two additional dimensions can be useful to complement the paternalistic leadership style: benevolent leadership which cares for the skill development of their subordinates to boost initiative and creativity, and moral leadership which treats subordinates with respect and trust, which together empower employees psychologically and professionally (Gyamerah, S., 2022).

Culture to Transform Hearts

The above 4Cs should be embedded in a broader organisational culture for them to flourish and drive real transformations. Leaders play a crucial role in driving the culture change.

I observe, however, three major blockers of cultural change within public organisations.

First, awareness is lacking of an organisational culture in the public sector. The only prevalent "culture" of most state-owned enterprises (SOEs), if any, consists of stability, uniformity and predictability. However, creating a culture that supports the goals and objectives is an important factor in the effectiveness of SOEs.

Secondly, culture often remains an empty mantra that leaders purport in words; rather, it should be translated into actions and institutions. For example, when a leader wants to promote a culture of inter-departmental teamwork, he can institutionalise monthly meetings for members of different departments to exchange insights. If no institutional changes are made, cultural change will remain transient and abstract.

Thirdly, organisational culture should be symbiotic with the broader societal values. National culture plays an important role in shaping organisational culture (Dickson, 2004). Arbitrary transplantation of Western corporate culture in an organisation operating in an Oriental society may provoke considerable friction, if not resistance. For example, humility and reverence have been important virtues of the Chinese culture for thousands of years. As we say, the moon waxes only to wane, the water surges only to overflow (月满则亏，水满则溢). In such a culture, it is common in meetings to see employees not speak up and not exalt achievements. I think in this case the best approach is to have routine office hours to speak privately with staff and take monthly pulse surveys to establish feedback channels from staff to make their voices heard. Leaders must grasp the deep-rooted national culture before initiating meaningful changes in the organisational culture.

References

Bar-On, Reuven, & Parker, James. D. A. *The Handbook of Emotional Intelligence*. San Francisco, CA: Jossey-Bass Inc, 2000.

Bessant, John, High Involvement Innovation, https://www.linkedin.com/pulse/every-pair-hands-you-get-free-brain-john-bessant.

Dickson, Marcus, BeShears, Renee, & Gupta, Vipin. "The Impact of Societal Culture and Industry on Organizational Culture. In *Culture, Leadership and Organization: The Globe Study of 62 Societies*, edited by R. J. House, P. J. Hanges, M. Javidan, P. W. Dorfman & V. Gupta. Thousand Oaks, CA: Sage Publications, Inc., 74-87, 2004.

Edmondson, Amy C. *The Fearless Organization: Creating Psychological Safety in the Workplace for Learning, Innovation, and Growth*. Wiley, 2018.

Gentry, William. A., Weber, Todd J., & Golnaz, Sadri. "Empathy in the Workplace: A Tool for Effective Leadership" [White paper]. Center for Creative Leadership, 2016. https://doi.org/10.35613/ccl.2016.1070.

Gyamerah, Samuel, He, Zheng, Asante, Dennis, Ampaw, Enock M., & Gyamerah, Emmanuel. E. D. "Paternalistic Leadership, Employee Creativity, and Retention: The Role of Psychological Empowerment", *International Journal of Cross-Cultural Management*, Vol. 22, No. 1 (2022), pp. 83-104. https://doi.org/10.1177/14705958221081636.

Lordan, Grace. "Courage and Leadership in 2023", London School of Economics, January 4, 2023.

Mehrabian, Albert, *Silent Messages: Implicit Communication of Emotions and Attitudes*. Wadsworth Publishing, 1971.

Northouse, Peter G. *Leadership: Theory and Practice*. Sage, 2013.

Novogratz, Jacqueline, & McNulty, Anne W. "The Most Critical Ingredient in Leadership", *Stanford Social Innovation Review* (July 6, 2022).

Shamir, Boas, House, Robert J., & Arthur, Michael. B. "The Motivational Effects of Charismatic Leadership: A Self-concept Based Theory", *Organization Science*, Vol. 4, No. 4 (2013), pp. 577-594.

Stone, Deborah A. "Causal Stories and the Formation of Policy Agendas", *Political Science Quarterly*, Vol. 104, No. 2 (Summer, 1989), pp. 281-300.

Strange, Jill M., & Mumford, Michael D. "The Origins of Vision: Charismatic Versus Ideological Leadership", *The Leadership Quarterly*, Vol. 13, No. 4 (2002), pp. 343-377.

Case Study on Managing Change
Bill Bratton and NYPD Take on Crime in New York City

(In my MPP/MPA class, I regularly discuss the case of how NYC Police Commissioner William Bratton transformed NYPD and took on crime in NYC. I mostly use John Kotter's eight-step change model to explain how Bratton managed the change. We could also look at the case using the 5Cs framework. Bratton had the clarity of his vision. He understood the importance of dealing with broken windows. He had the courage to transform the Police Force and tackle corruption. He knew how to communicate to members of the Force as well as the public and other stakeholders. He cared for his people. He understood the power of organisational culture.)

*T*IME magazine 15 January 1996 had on its cover a photo of William Bratton, with the following headline: "Finally, we are winning the war against crime. Here's why".

Who is Bill Bratton? Born in Boston in 1947, he joined the Boston Police Department in 1970, rising to become its top uniformed officer in 1980. In 1983, he was made Police Chief of the Massachusetts Bay Transportation Authority and in 1990, he became New York City Transit Police chief. In January 1992, he moved back to the Boston Police

Department as its Number Two, becoming Boston Police Commissioner in March 1993. When Rudy Giuliani was elected New York City Mayor in November 1993 on a strong anti-crime platform, Bratton lobbied for the job and was appointed New York City Police Commissioner in January 1994.

Crime had grown so far out of control in NYC that the press referred to the Big Apple as the Rotten Apple. Yet in less than two years, and without an increase in his budget, Bratton turned New York into the safest large city in the nation. Between 1994 and 1996, felony crime fell 39%, murders 50% and theft 35%. Gallup polls reported that public confidence in the NYPD jumped from 37% to 73%, while internal surveys showed job satisfaction in the Police Department reaching an all-time high.

How did Bratton do it?

First, there was a sense of urgency. Giuliani had won the NYC Mayor elections emphasising quality of life issues. Reducing crime was the mayor's pre-eminent priority.

Second, Bratton was able to gather a top team to support his objective. The team comprised a mix of people who had worked with him in previous organisations as well as new NYPD colleagues. Bratton welcomed diversity to his team, was open minded and creative in using talents.

Bratton's team included:

- George Kelling, a criminologist and academic who developed the "Broken Windows" theory with James Wilson, and whom Bratton knew earlier at NYC Transit Police when Kelling was then hired as a consultant.

- John Linder, a skillful communicator, who was introduced to Bratton by Kelling. Linder was then a consultant and Bratton engaged him to conduct cultural diagnostics of the NYPD and suggest ways of energising the NYPD. Being new to the NYPD, it was important to Bratton that he understood the culture in the NYPD.

- Jack Maple, previously Head of Central Robbery Squad, NYC Transit Police with Bratton, became Deputy Commissioner for Crime Control Strategies in NYC. Quirky but brilliant and innovative, Maple was described by *The New Yorker* in February 1997 as follows: "In 1981, when he was still making twenty-odd thousand dollars a year, Jack walked into the Money Store and, using his house in Queens as collateral, got a home-equity loan for twenty thousand dollars. He spent the money in large part, at the Plaza and on clothing." How many bosses would dare employ such a quirky character? Bratton did because he recognised Maple's talents and indeed most of the successful anti-crime initiatives, including CompStat, were Maple's ideas.

- Peter LaPorte, previously Chief of Staff to Boston Police Commissioner Bratton, became Chief of Staff to NYC Police Commissioner Bratton.

- John Miller, from WNBC and close to the Giuliani camp, became Deputy Commissioner for Public Information.

Bratton knew the importance of understanding the plotting, intrigue and politics involved in pushing through change. Powerful vested interests would resist the impending reforms, especially in an organisation such as the NYPD. He understood he had to have respected senior insiders on the top team. He promoted and included several capable senior NYPD officers in his guiding coalition, including those who were strong supporters of the previous NYC Police Commissioner.

The promotions were not necessarily based on seniority.

- John Timoney, a one star was promoted to Chief of Department, NYPD's highest uniformed officer, passing over 16 higher-ranking officers.
- Louis Anemone, a field general like "Patton", was made Chief of Patrol.
- David Scott, previously Chief of Department, a long-time veteran of the NYPD, an African American, was made first Deputy Police Commissioner.

Third, creating a vision. Bratton had a 40% crime reduction in three years, with 10% in the first year. This was an audacious goal. To make the challenge seem manageable, Bratton framed it as a series of specific goals that officers at different levels could relate to. As he put it, the challenge the NYPD faced was to make the streets of New York safe "block by block, precinct by precinct, and borough by borough".

He also mapped out the strategy for his department to achieve. He issued Crime Control Strategies to guide the men to do their job:

#1: Getting Guns off the Streets

#2: Curbing Youth Violence in Schools and Streets

#3: Driving Drug Dealers Out

#4: Breaking Cycles of Domestic Violence

#5: Reclaiming Public Spaces.

He sought to re-energise the Police Department through:

1. Quality of life policing
2. Assertive policing

3. Devolving authority

- *Getting rid of obstacles to change* – replacing four out of the five NYPD's super chiefs
- *Devolving power* to the 76 precinct commanders – every precinct commander to function as a mini police chief
- *Enhance authority* of precinct commanders –
  - » Detectives to report to precinct commanders and not just to the detective bureau of HQ
  - » Precinct commanders to run their own anti-vice ops
- *Accountability* – measuring crime and twice weekly meetings at 7am

4. Psychological touch

He communicated the vision well.

Consolidating improvements and producing still more changes and instituting new approaches, Bratton, or more accurately Maple, introduced CompStat. As outlined by Maple, the principles of controlling crime are:

1. Accurate and timely intelligence
2. Rapid deployment
3. Responding using effective tactics
4. Relentless follow-up and assessment

Compstat is a way to animate these four principles.

Precinct commanders had to explain projected maps and charts that showed, based on the CompStat data, the precinct's patterns of crimes and when and where the police responded. They would be required to provide a detailed explanation if police activity did not mirror crime spikes, and would also be asked how officers were addressing the precinct's issues and why performance was improving or deteriorating. The meetings allowed Bratton and his senior staff to carefully monitor and assess how well commanders were motivating and managing their people and how well they were focusing on strategic hot spots.

A February 1996 interview with American talk show host Charlie Rose was revealing:

"Charlie Rose: Some say what you have done is to put the fear of God in your precinct commanders by setting very tough standards for them, which basically says, deliver on reducing crime or you may not be here.

"Bill Bratton: Deliver on reducing crime or have a reason why you cannot. And then we as an organisation will collectively work with you. The biggest way or the easiest way to fall from grace in the NYPD is to not have a plan, not to understand what is going on in your precinct and not to have a plan to address it, and then if with the resources you have available, your plan doesn't work, then we'll work with you as an organisation. People that have been removed from command, and there have been a lot of them, it hasn't been as much for the failure to reduce crime or improve quality of life, it's the idea that not being able to generate creative plans to deal with the problem."

Leaders are key. Singapore's Prime Minister Lee Kuan Yew in his 1984 National Day Rally Speech said:

"Everything works, whether it's water, electricity, gas, telephone, telexes, it just has to work. If it doesn't work, I want to know why, and if I am not satisfied, and I often was not, the chief goes, and I have to find another chief. Firing a chief is very simple. Getting one who will do the job better is a different matter. And the critical factor is confidence. Confidence of the people, not just your own citizens. But confidence of foreign investors, foreign government. Confidence that there is a government in Singapore that will act swiftly, rationally and often predictably."

Bratton's change method can be analysed using John Kotter's Change Model, which has eight steps as follows:

1. Step One: Create a Sense of Urgency
2. Step Two: Build a Powerful Guiding Coalition
3. Step Three: Form a Strategic Vision and Initiatives
4. Step Four: Enlist a Volunteer Army (Communicate the Vision)
5. Step Five: Enable Action by Removing the Barriers
6. Step Six: Generate Short-Term Wins
7. Step Seven: Sustain Acceleration (Build on the Change)
8. Step Eight: Institute Change (Anchor the Changes in Corporate Culture)

(Read John Kotter, "Leading Change: Why Transformation Efforts Fail", *Harvard Business Review*, May 1995. Additional Reading: "Accelerate!" *Harvard Business Review*, Nov 2012.)

Kotter's change model is useful. I have used it with some modification when I need to lead major change. Kotter subsequently wrote *The Heart of Change* (HBR Press, 2002) because he realised that the single biggest challenge in the process is changing people's behaviour. The key to this behavioural shift, so clear in successful transformations, is less about analysis and thinking and more about seeing and feeling. People are sensitive to the emotions that undermine/facilitate change, and they will find ways to reduce/enhance those feelings: <u>see-feel-change</u>.

The 'Broken Windows' Debate

The theory, introduced in 1982, states that maintaining order could reduce the incidence of serious crimes. "Consider a building with a few broken windows," wrote James Q. Wilson, a government professor at Harvard University, and George L. Kelling, a criminal justice professor at Rutgers University. "If the windows are not repaired, the tendency is for vandals to break a few more windows. Eventually, they may even break into the building, and if it's unoccupied, perhaps become squatters or light fires inside." Disorder, in other words, led to serious crime. Wilson and Kelling posed a revolutionary theory: If the original windows were repaired, the escalating string of crimes that followed might be checked before it began. Their theory has been celebrated as the driving force behind a historic reduction in crime in New York City in the 1990s. It is also been questioned by many sociologists and criminologists, and associated with controversial policing practices such as New York's "stop-and-frisk" programme.

How much of NYC's crime problem could be solved through better policing, and how much must be solved, instead, through social reform?

Crimes are offences against society, but, when they become pervasive enough, they can gain a new meaning, and become criticisms of it. Addressing the root causes of poverty, racism and social injustices is important.

San Francisco experienced a homeless crisis. In fact, it was so bad that it was widely reported by global media that city leaders had pushed for a clean-up ahead of the Asia-Pacific Economic Cooperation (APEC) Leaders' meeting and the anticipated Biden-Xi meeting in November 2023. What had gone wrong? Is the homelessness problem caused by poverty, lack of housing or is it caused by addiction, mental illness and "disaffiliation"? Or is it due to the state law that holds that stealing merchandise worth $950 or less is just a misdemeanour, which means that law enforcement probably will not bother to investigate, and if they do, prosecutors will let it go.

Leading the change is often not just within the organisation. There is also the need to lead the change with the public. Public service leaders must understand they operate within their organisation as well as beyond their organisation.

Political leadership is foremost. In the case of NYC, Bratton needed the support of Mayor Giuliani. Public servants serve the people and help political leaders achieve the results desired by the people. It is the political leaders who have the mandate of the people.

What happened to Bill Bratton?

- Resigned in 1996 partly due to Giuliani's belief that Bratton was getting more credit for the reduction in crime than Giuliani
- Worked as a private consultant with Kroll Associates
- Appointed LAPD Chief of Police in 2002

- Approached by British Prime Minister David Cameron in 2011 to become the new Metropolitan Police Commissioner. However, it did not happen as the Home Affairs Secretary did not agree due to objections by senior British Police Officers.
- Returned to NYC as Police Commissioner, 2014-2016.

Bratton revealed in an interview with CNBC Make It on what his "biggest mistake" taught him about ambition (https://www.cnbc.com/2018/07/12/bill-bratton-reveals-what-his-biggest-mistake-taught-him-about-manag.html). An excerpt from the article is presented below.

"I regretted that, I still regret it," Bratton says of his ending with Giuliani. "The mistake I made with the mayor was, using the term, I didn't 'stay in his headlights' – I didn't stay close enough to him and to his vision."

The takeaway – that balancing personal ambition and a boss' vision can be difficult – reinforced an earlier experience Bratton had when he was just making a name for himself on Boston's Police Force. Having been promoted to the Boston Police Department's number-two position in 1980, Bratton was interviewed for his first big magazine profile.

"I commented that someday I'd like to be the police commissioner," he recalls. "The sitting police commissioner at that time took some offense at that, and within about a year I was gone. So sometimes, you know, you have to really be very mindful of your audience when you make comments or make projections, because not all ears hear it the same way."

"I worked very hard working for the next three mayors I worked for to stay within their headlights," Bratton says. *"Leadership, sometimes, is the idea that you're the lone wolf, if you will, but oftentimes leadership is also learning to stay within the parameters of those that you are working for – other leaders."*

References

Kotter, John, *"Leading Change"*, *Harvard Business Review,* January 2007 (originally 1995).

"Assertive Policing, Plummeting Crime: The NYPD Takes on Crime in New York City", Harvard Kennedy School Case 1999.

CHAPTER 11

The Power of Character

L ife will always throw curve balls, stumbling blocks and obstacles. Persevere at overcoming them and learn to triumph over life's imperfections. Most of all, stay true to your values. Do what is right. Character, more than anything else, will shape your values, judgement and destiny.

People must believe that their leader can be trusted. Trust that he will deliver the vision and promised results. Trust that he has their interests and welfare at heart. That he tells the truth. Better if he can tell hard truths.

The leader must have integrity. Integrity is a fundamental required of the leader.

The leader is responsible for ensuring standards of moral and ethical conduct. He must engage in ethically correct behaviour, regardless of pressure.

Integrity is needed when deciding on what action needs to be taken. What is the right thing to do?

How to live a life of integrity – and stay out of jail.

In his book *How Will You Measure Your Life?* (HBR Press, 2017), Professor Clayton Christensen explained why focusing on marginal costs and revenues can lead to personal, professional and moral failure:

"The marginal cost of doing something 'just this once' always seems to be negligible, but the full cost will typically be much higher. Yet unconsciously, we will naturally employ the marginal-cost doctrine in our personal lives. A voice in our head says, 'Look, I know that as a general rule, most people shouldn't do this. But in this particular extenuating circumstance, just this once, it's okay.'

"Nick Leeson, the twenty-six-year-old trader who famously brought down British merchant bank Barings in 1995 after racking up $1.3 billion in trading losses before being detected, talks about how marginal thinking led him down an inconceivable path. As Barings realized the extent of Leeson's debt, it was forced to declare bankruptcy. The bank was sold to ING for just 1 pound. Twelve hundred employees lost their jobs, some of them his friends. And Leeson was sentenced to six and a half years in a Singaporean prison."

Decide what you stand for. And then stand for it all the time: Holding to your principles 100% of the time is easier than 98% of the time.

Integrity is a Potential Blind Spot of Serious Concern

A 2016 Center for Creative Leadership paper ("The Irony of Integrity: A Study of the Character Strengths of Leaders") finds that integrity is the most important contributor to top-level executives' current performance. However, it went on:

"What's more troubling, C-suite executives may not know they have problems with integrity when they get their C-suite office. The top-level executives in its study overrated their integrity in comparison to ratings of their integrity provided by their direct reports. Unfortunately, they may be out-of-touch with how they are perceived because of the continual success they achieved during their career to these top-level positions. No doubt, success breeds confidence. But, there is a fine line between confidence and arrogance, which may make a leader unapproachable."

Congruence Between Values and Action

What is important is that leaders must be congruent in their personal and professional lives, to enhance their credibility and inspire their people to follow their lead. When a leader's actions align with his words, it creates a culture of trust, respect and accountability within the organisation. They are who they say they are, and they do what they say they do. Authenticity. Not fake.

Competence

The leader must prove himself competent. Leadership competence is being affected by rapid technological advancement, a more volatile operating environment and an unpredictable global situation. He must continually upskill and update knowledge; adapt and integrate into technological changes at work; form strong networks and powerful coalitions; understand cultural differences; be innovative and creative in problem solving; and work hard and work smart.

Question: How do you operate in an increasingly complex/chaotic environment?

Achieving results will often depend on intangibles, such as luck and circumstances. There must be resilience to overcome setbacks and tenacity to pursue goals.

Summary

A leader may demonstrate exceptional leadership qualities based on the 5Cs. But if his professional and personal lives are irreconcilable, he will not be regarded as a truly good leader. In fact, he will eventually not succeed. The leader must incorporate the 5Cs in a consistent and authentic way. Character remains key.

How to Be a Good Leader

Tommy Koh

I wish to thank my good friend, Tan Yong Soon, for inviting me to contribute a short essay on leadership.

I want to begin by talking about the kinds of leaders that I dislike.

I dislike the dictatorial leader. A dictatorial leader is one who does not consult his colleagues. He seeks to impose his views. He doesn't tolerate dissent. Very often, the dictatorial leader is also bad-tempered. He will use his anger to intimidate others.

The second kind of leader I dislike is the weak leader. He lacks self-confidence and is often confused. He is reluctant to take decisions. He allows some of his colleagues to push him around.

The third kind of leader I dislike is one who leads by playing favourites. Instead of unifying his team, delegation or conference, he divides them by empowering his favourites. The consequence is division and low morale.

From a very young age, I have been entrusted with leadership positions. In Singapore, I was the Dean of the National University of Singapore (NUS) Law School; head of the Institute of Policy Studies, a think tank; Rector of Tembusu College at NUS; chairman of the National Arts Council and the National Heritage Board. I was also the leader of a delegation which negotiated a free trade agreement with the United States of America, and of another delegation which negotiated with the People's Republic of China on an agreement to establish diplomatic relations between our two countries.

At the United Nations (UN), I was entrusted to chair the Third UN Conference on the Law of the Sea and the UN Conference on Environment and Development, also known as the Earth Summit.

How to be a good leader? These are some of the rules which I have observed in my work. First, master your brief. There is no substitute for hard work. You should try to know your brief or the documents being negotiated better than your colleagues. By doing so, you will establish your credibility.

Second, unite your delegation or conference by your humility, sincerity and goodwill. Treat everyone with respect and kindness. Give responsibility to your more capable colleagues but do not disrespect the others. Everyone must feel that he is valued and has been treated with fairness.

Third, a good leader must be optimistic and have a never-say-die attitude. It is normal to encounter challenges and difficulties. Sometimes you may even encounter a crisis. When that happens, the leader must remain calm and stable. He must remain optimistic and think of creative solutions to the challenges.

Fourth, be a consultative leader. Everyone must feel that his view has been taken into account. However, when the time is ripe to decide, a good leader must have the courage to act boldly and confidently.

Fifth, a good leader must be able to write clearly. He must also be able to speak clearly and persuasively. The ability to communicate well, both orally and in writing, is a necessary skill of a good leader. You cannot be a good leader if you are unable to communicate your thoughts to others and to persuade them to agree with your view.

ABOUT TOMMY KOH

Tommy Koh is Ambassador-at-Large at the Ministry of Foreign Affairs, Singapore. He had served as Dean of the Faculty of Law of NUS, Chairman of the National Arts Council, Chairman of the National Heritage Board, Singapore's Permanent Representative to the United Nations (UN) in New York and Ambassador to the United States of America. He was President of the Third UN Conference on the Law of the Sea. He was also the Chairman of the Preparatory Committee for and the Main Committee of the UN Conference on Environment and Development (Earth Summit). In 2006, he was awarded Champion of the Earth, UN's highest environmental honour. In 2014, he received the Great Negotiator Award from Program on Negotiation at Harvard Law School.

Musings on Leadership

Chua Chin Kiat

Introduction

Many people who know about the Singapore prison reform that started in 1999 credited me with transforming the prison system from one that locked people up to one that reformed the prison inmates. In truth, such a feat could not be pulled off by an individual. What I did was an act of leadership galvanising the whole of the Prison Service to turn things around. Since this essay is about leadership, let me summarise the prison reform process before sharing my musings.

At the beginning of my tenure in the Prison Service, it was a matter of change or die. The prisons then were built to house 5,000 inmates, but the prison population was three times the design capacity. We were sitting on a powder keg that could explode at any time. The Prison Service of course will always exist, but those of us at the helm who failed to deal with the crisis would surely suffer early career termination and tarnished reputations if the prisons careened into the abyss of prison riots with loss of lives. So reform was almost a no-brainer.

The process we went through to avert the crisis and transform the system can be summarised as follows:

- Stabilise the situation by seeking quick wins
- Re-think and re-frame the desired future by visioning
- Re-formulate new mental models to realise the vision
- Re-invent new strategies and systemic structures
- Re-learn and review to stay relevant

My role as the leader throughout this process was at times pivotal. I had to ask tough questions, model the desired behaviour and foster teamwork. However, if we know our physics, a pivot doesn't get the work done, the rest of the fulcrum does.

Before we talk about leadership, let us first be clear what leadership is. I will start by asking the question "What are the fundamentals of leadership?" Stripped to its bare bones, leadership really only consists of two elements: followers and a destination. Leadership is the process of taking the followers to the desired destination. A leader is not a leader if he has no followers. He will have no followers if he cannot describe a destination, a place, a state of being or a treasure that people would like to reach or attain and that he can lead them to. So the fundamentals of leadership are to prepare your descriptions of that destination and go find your followers.

Leadership is About the Future

Employers are not necessarily leaders. Between employers and employees, the relationship is often more like that between the contractor and the contracted. An employer gives a certain set of tasks to the employee to accomplish at a certain contracted rate. In other words, if you do your tasks as required, you will be paid a certain amount. I may be the employer of my domestic helper but I am not leading her anywhere. Sometimes, as in the case of a maid agency, maids are not employees of the agency. They are again re-contracted out to clients and take instructions from them. Quite clearly, the maids will not see the agency as their leader.

Another good illustration of this is the building trade. A bricklayer lays bricks and gets paid for that. He may occasionally be given other tasks he is able to do within the scope of the building trade, but that is all within the understanding of the contractor and the bricklayer. Typically, there is no leadership involved in this relationship. This relationship changes immediately if the bricklayer is promised a promotion, a pay increase or a skill upgrade if he does his job well and meets certain targets or passes certain assessments. There is now a future for the bricklayer to look forward to, something he wants to attain. Never mind whether the contractor is sincere in offering those future rewards. The contractor is now more than a contractor. He is someone whose instructions to do additional tasks – even if it is outside the scope of the original job description – must be obeyed for the realisation of that promise.

There are a few things that we have established in this example. Firstly, leadership is about a promise of the future and not about the here and now. Secondly, that future has to be clear both to the leader and the follower. Otherwise, in time to come, if that future remains unclear or perceived to be unattainable, no matter how enticing the promise is, the follower will go and find some other leader. Thirdly, if that future happens to be a part of the leader's aspiration too, then the leader needs to motivate his followers to stick to him and help him to attain that future together. It follows that if you are a leader, the all-important people are your followers and the all-important thing is that desired future.

Leadership is About Followers

When I was still in service, I made a habit of meeting the graduating class of the senior officers' course over lunch. One question I often asked the graduands was why they wanted to become leaders. Most said that they could then do greater things. Many said that they could make a greater contribution to society. Some honest ones even said they could then retire more comfortably. None of these young men and women understood that leadership was not about themselves, but about the cause they chose and their followers. That is why I want to make this absolutely clear, especially to aspiring young leaders.

Leadership therefore comprises the interactions between leaders and followers. Leadership is a process. Every little one-time interaction makes up that process and the purpose of the process is to attain the desired future. Successful leadership then is the ability to manage every interaction with the followers such that the followers continue to believe that the desired future is enticing and attainable and they continue to want to go there. If a leader is not sincere in bringing his followers to the promised desired future for the sake of the followers, he will soon be found out and his quest will have few followers. Ultimately, his quest will fall short.

Much of the time, what we think as leadership is not leadership at all. For example, supervision is not leadership. The contractor may employ a supervisor over the bricklayer to ensure that the bricklayer does as he is contracted to do. The bricklayer will be somewhat wary of the supervisor because he has the power to make his life difficult. But that does not make the supervisor his leader. If the supervisor does not handle his interactions with the bricklayer properly, the bricklayer will soon find another contractor. Management is not leadership. Management is typically concerned with the disposition of resources to accomplish goals set for the managers. A manager is a leader only if he is also given the job of managing the journey of the employees under them to reach the desired future. The use of managers in the leadership process also demonstrates that leadership is not a sole proprietorship. Interactions with a representative of the leader in the shape of the manager constitute part of the leadership process.

To summarise, good leadership is the art of managing every interaction with followers well enough so that their desire to attain the common goal or destination is continually reinforced. Of course this way of looking at leadership is rather over-simplified but it is fundamental to understanding the basics of leadership. I often asked myself what confers a person the right to be a leader. The answer is not as obvious as it seems. Many people are put in leadership positions by a higher authority. The higher authority presumably assesses that they have the leadership qualities before conferring them the positions, but this is not always the case. Some other considerations intrude. For example, the higher authority may have wanted his own kin or someone he can absolutely trust to occupy those positions, never mind whether the candidate has the right qualities or not. Some such leaders actually grow in their job and learn their craft. If they don't, they will become failed leaders. In some situations, natural leaders emerge to take charge. For example, in mining accidents when some miners were trapped together underground, frequently one of them would emerge to organise and lead the group so that they had the best chance of survival. Not all such episodes had a happy ending. For those that had a happy ending, the leader's role was often vital. So what is that leadership quality?

Ability to See Farther

First of all, a person has the right to lead because he sees farther than all the others. He is able to anticipate what is around the next corner better than those he leads. In other words, he is the most strategic thinker in the team he leads. There are various ways in which this person is described: visionary, wise, sound, having a good mind and so on. To me, the common denominator of all these descriptions is having a longer time horizon than all his followers. He sees farther ahead and he sees more. Part of this ability comes from nurture. Experience and training sharpen the ability in some people to recognise patterns that will lead to a certain outcome. The other part of course comes from nature. That is why experience and training do nothing for some people. So the ability to learn is key to developing a longer time horizon. Different readers who read my essay will take away different things and some will take away nothing, except that it is boring. Good leaders are all naturally curious and keen learners. No visionaries have completely original visions. They all draw a good part of it from someone else.

Another quite important component of the leadership quality is the ability to communicate. A good communicator touches emotions and engenders actions. Again, this component is partly nature and partly nurture. Some will never have it no matter how much media training they undergo. Some are naturals at it but training will surely sharpen them. Without nurture, nature will not take its course!

The Importance of Humility and Faith

The other important component is the ability to keep an open mind in order to garner as many possible courses of action as possible. This in turn offers the best chance of selecting the correct course of action. When a course of action is decided upon, one must then focus doggedly on the objective and pursue it. To put it more profoundly, a leader must be humble enough to listen to others (i.e., able to learn) but faithful enough to stay the course and be dictated by his moral principles.

During the reform process of the Prison Service, when the going got tough, I often reminded my people that "faith energises and fear paralyses". To stay on course, a leader must believe in the rightness of what he is doing and thus block the invasion of fear into his conscious mind.

Rightness of a cause does not come from pursuing personal glory. It comes from pursuing the common good. The followers will follow the leader because they know that he has their interests at heart and is willing to make sacrifices for their interests. So getting down to brass tacks, leadership quality is the ability to learn, communicate and keep the faith.

Conclusion

Let me conclude by saying that leadership is like priesthood. Not everyone is cut out for it. It calls for a lot of self-discipline and self-sacrifice for the common good; quite a bit of it is innate. If you are not cut out for it, the next best thing to do is to be a good follower and do the real work. That can be just as exciting as being a leader.

ABOUT CHUA CHIN KIAT

Chua Chin Kiat held key appointments in the Ministry of Home Affairs Headquarters (Director of Operations) and the Singapore Police Force (Director of Manpower, Director of Operations and Director of Criminal Investigation Department). He was the Director of Prisons from 1 November 1998 to 31 October 2007. He helped transformed the Prison Service from a custody-focused mindset to a rehabilitation-centred culture and drastically brought the recidivism rate of prisoners down.

Indonesia's Public Sector in a Challenging Time: Promoting Reforms, Addressing Uncertainties

Yanuar Nugroho

Indonesia, Southeast Asia's largest economy, presents a unique canvas marked by its diverse population, sprawling archipelago and dynamic political landscape. The public sector plays a crucial role in the country's development, particularly in providing essential services, ensuring governance and facilitating economic growth. However, Indonesia faces numerous challenges in an era characterised by rapid technological advancements, a shifting geopolitical landscape, worsening climate and planetary crises, as well as evolving social norms globally. Nationally, political dynamics following the recent 2024 election also pose challenges in terms of governance and state capacity.

In this context, the public sector's efficiency is often hindered by bureaucratic inefficiency, corruption and resource allocation issues. As global standards evolve and domestic demands increase, there is a pressing need for comprehensive reforms tailored to enhance responsiveness and effectiveness. It is against this backdrop that promoting reform in Indonesia's public sector is key to addressing uncertainties[1] during these constantly changing times. This short contribution explores a few key cases of reform, both in the past and in aspirations for the future, those that work or otherwise. It is hoped that sharing these cases of reform might offer some valuable insights and lessons learned.

Promoting Reform Amidst Bureaucratic Inertia

One of the primary challenges in reforming the Indonesian bureaucracy – with more than four million state civil apparatuses – is inertia which manifests in a chronic symptom: the so-called "sectoral ego". This means a siloed bureaucracy that is often unwilling to share resources, overemphasising hierarchy and discouraging risk-taking and innovations. This symptom of inertia impedes the implementation of necessary reforms that require adaptability and quick decision-making which is crucial in responding to future uncertainties – like the COVID-19 pandemic that nearly paralysed the country.

Among the few key breakthroughs to address this symptom is the establishment of e-government (Presidential Regulation No. 95/2018) that binds and strengthens earlier initiatives: One Data Indonesia (Pres Reg No. 39/2019) and One Map Policy (Pres Reg No. 9/2016 revised into No. 23/2021). This is aimed at improving bureaucracy efficiency through digital transformation

---

[1]   In this essay, the word "uncertainty" is simply used to express the world that is VUCA – vulnerable, uncertain, complex and ambiguous – and, after the pandemic we realised, BANI – brittle, anxious, non-linear and incomprehensible.

and services. Despite some successes – particularly in advancing accuracy of social protection targeting through CRVS (Civil Registry and Vital Statistics) and ministerial data integration – overall achievement would be contingent upon transforming the bureaucratic mindset and adopting new technologies across all levels of government.

Yet, digital transformation in the public sector comes with two main challenges: cybersecurity and data privacy. As Indonesia adopts more digital solutions, it becomes increasingly vulnerable to cyberattacks, which can cripple essential services and leak sensitive information. Developing robust cybersecurity protocols and continuously updating them in line with global standards is crucial for safeguarding public data and ensuring the reliability of digital public services. In addition to e-government and digital transformation, talent management for the civil service was also designed to encourage the best people to join the public sector to equip the government in embracing the future challenges. This includes reforms in civil service formation: from recruitment, training and placement to deployment and career development – both at the central and sub-national governments. Such reform was also intended to de-politicise bureaucracy that had been politicised for quite a long time. Although bureaucracy is ultimately very close to – and cannot be separated from – politics, politicisation of bureaucracy would never help reform it.

Addressing Rampant Corruption

Corruption remains a pervasive issue, undermining trust and efficiency in the public sector. Post-Reformasi, the Corruption Eradication Commission (KPK) was established as an independent state institution in 2003. Yet, high-profile corruption cases that often involve politicians and public servants suggest a systemic problem that extends beyond individual misdeeds. As such, in the future, as more things become uncertain, ironically corruption might be the only certain thing characterising public sector performance. For this, a breakthrough was set up: the initiation of the National Strategy for the Prevention of Corruption (Stranas PK) (Pres Reg No. 55/2012, revised No. 54/2018) that was aimed at strengthening legal frameworks, enhancing transparency, and fostering a public service culture that prioritises integrity as essential steps towards preventing and mitigating corruption. The strategy seemed to have worked: the Corruption Perception Index score increased between 2012 and 2019 before it dropped in 2020, and continued to do so until 2023 due to one thing – the weakening of the KPK. The KPK was made part of the government under the President in 2019, losing its independence. Since then, there has been a credible worry that corruption would only be more and more rampant in the future. This is a huge task for the new government: to restore public trust in its commitment to fight against corruption.

Resource Allocation and Decentralisation

One major reform in the public sector since the 1998 reform is decentralisation of administrative powers to local governments. It was intended to make governance more responsive to local needs. However, this has also led to uneven resource distribution and varying levels of public service quality across regions. Remote areas, especially in underdeveloped regions such as eastern

Indonesia, often struggle with inadequate infrastructure and limited access to basic services. Balancing resource allocation, ensuring equitable development and providing adequate training for local officials are critical for addressing these disparities. This requires the strengthening of state capacity, i.e., the ability to administer and deliver development both at the national and sub-national governments particularly in the dimensions of public administration and provision of essential services.

A study of two decades of decentralisation in Indonesia (Nugroho & Sujarwoto, 2021)[2] reveals that in Indonesia, overall state capacity in delivering public services improved under decentralisation. This was probably due to the increase in the quality of public administration at the sub-national level. However, disparities and gaps among regions are also evident, particularly those in Java-Bali and outside Java-Bali and eastern Indonesia. The study also reveals that decentralisation has made policy coordination between central and sub-national governments in delivering development more complex, due to the high level of political intervention at both levels. Clearly decentralisation is inevitable for a country as big and diverse as Indonesia; yet the way it is implemented also needs reform. Such reform is crucial as decentralisation must help the government to navigate uncertainties stemming from global and national shifts in economy, social and political dynamics – even climate and environmental changes.

---

[2]   Yanuar Nugroho and Sujarwoto (2021), Institutions, Outputs, and Outcomes: Two Decades of Decentralization and State Capacity in Indonesia, *Journal of Southeast Asian Economies*, Vol. 38, No. 3, pp. 296-319.

Concluding Remarks

Indonesia's journey towards a reformed and resilient public sector is fraught with challenges that require innovative solutions and steadfast governance. Promoting reform in the bureaucracy, combating corruption and decentralising government are key in adapting to global changes and are imperative for Indonesia to navigate successfully through constantly changing times. These reforms are not only about policy adjustments but also entail a cultural shift towards transparency, efficiency and adaptability. This way, the government would be able to create policies that are flexible and resilient, allowing for quick adaptation to global market changes, shocks and disasters, or shifts in socio-economic-political dynamics. Only by confronting these challenges head-on can Indonesia ensure a robust public sector that not only survives but also thrives in the face of global and domestic future uncertainties.

ABOUT YANUAR NUGROHO

Yanuar Nugroho, PhD, is a scholar and public policy practitioner. After returning from the UK as a Research Fellow at the University of Manchester from 2004-2012, he served as a Director then Deputy Chief of Staff at the Executive Office of the President of Indonesia from 2012-2019. He was team leader for the monitoring and evaluation of the COVID Active Response and Expenditure Support in Indonesia 2020-2021, held a Senior Fellowship in Public Service at Lee Kuan Yew School of Public Policy, Singapore in 2021, then from 2022 was appointed as the Expert Coordinator at the SDGs National Secretariat at the Ministry of National Development Planning, Indonesia. He is also a Visiting Senior Fellow at ISEAS-Yusof Ishak Institute Singapore and Senior Lecturer at Driyarkara School of Philosophy, Jakarta.

Leadership During Changes: Navigating New Horizons

Pum Huot

Introduction

The hard truth: "The only thing constant in life is change"

This essay explores the importance of adaptability and resilience in leadership, emphasising that leaders must not only embrace change as an option but also recognise it as a fundamental aspect of their roles. Effective leaders are not just adherent to set procedures but also capable of overseeing and adjusting to changes and, more importantly, leading the change. These attributes are not only just ethical considerations but are also key tools in modern leadership in a constantly changing world.

Good changes versus bad changes

Leadership involves leading and managing changes in various ways, either positively influencing progress or negatively causing instability. Positive changes can boost efficiency, productivity and problem-solving, while negative changes can lead to resistance, confusion and decreased efficiency. Leaders must be able to distinguish and balance different types of changes, establishing conditions that foster good transitions while minimising the negative effects.

Why is change the greatest test of leadership?

Leadership during periods of transition inherently tests leaders as it questions the current state of affairs, pushes limits and demands a reconsideration of strategies and methods. Leaders must not only effectively initiate and manage change, but also motivate and inspire their followers to adjust to new circumstances. The Chinese philosopher Lao Tzu once said, "Water is fluid, soft and yielding; but the power of water is to wear away the rigid rock without any effort."[1] Lao Tzu's metaphor of water teaches leaders about adaptability and resilience. Water's fluidity and softness allow it to navigate resistance and gradually influence organisational cultures.

Effective leaders must understand existing norms, engage respectfully and make incremental changes. They must be adaptable, patient and persistent, emulating the softness of water. This philosophy challenges leaders to reassess their influence and navigate change effectively. A leader's ability to transform problems into opportunities for growth and innovation relies on a blend of vision, boldness and visionary thinking. The capacity

---

[1]   Tsai, Kuan Chen (2012). Lead the Way: Tao of Leadership. *Oriental Journal of Social Sciences*, Vol. 1, No. 1.

to guide and navigate through periods of change often distinguishes leaders who bring about significant and lasting transformations from those who simply oversee.

Challenges to Be Expected

The constant struggle between old norms and new change

Effective leaders adhere to the timeless advice of Sun Tzu, a Chinese philosopher who once said, "The wise warrior avoids the battle." When dealing with resistance to change, leaders minimise confrontations between old and new norms by utilising negotiation, strategic communication and empathy in order to align all parties with emerging objectives and approaches.[2] By understanding and addressing resistance, fear, misunderstanding or attachment with old norms. Promoting key innovations while upholding significant traditions enables leaders to honour the past and embrace the future, fostering an atmosphere that is open to change.

Change requires courage, determination and inspiration

Effective change execution requires realistic approaches, as well as individual attributes such as courage, resolution and motivation. Leaders must demonstrate these qualities to inspire people during times of change. They must take risks, persist with plans and gather team support. Leaders with these qualities facilitate transformation and cultivate a culture of adaptability and willingness within their teams.

---

[2] Griffith, Samuel B. (1963). *Sun Tzu: The Art of War*. Oxford University Press.

Changes are from within, not without

Internal evolution, rather than external pressure, is the most effective method for achieving durable and meaningful change within an organisation. Leaders who understand this cultivate a culture that supports ongoing improvement, recognising that successful transformations require aligning changes with the organisation's core principles. Such changes, when significant and aligned with foundational goals, are more likely to be sustained in the long term. This approach also reveals the limitations of superficial modifications made in response to external pressures, which often fail to address the root causes of negative perceptions and focus merely on image management.[3] Achieving lasting transformation necessitates a thorough analysis of the organisation's norms and decision-making processes, possibly requiring a challenging reassessment of core values to align the organisation's external actions with its true goals.

How to Navigate the Challenges

Embracing change is akin to mastering an art form. It demands a blend of meticulous strategy and audacious spirit, a character imbued with courage, determination and the ability to inspire others to welcome the winds of change. Indeed, not every leader is naturally equipped with the finesse to perfect this art.

---

[3]   Shank, Daniel B., & Burns, Alexander (2022). How Does Employees' Behavior Change How We Feel About Their Organization? Transfer of Affective Impressions Between Employees and Organizations. *Social Science Research*, 105.

Recognising the need for change

For many aspiring leaders, the acceptance of change hinges on its necessity. Whether the change is perceived as a necessity or merely a whim of the leader is a crucial determinant of successful transformation. Thus, a change-maker must discern if the proposed changes are genuinely needed and, equally important, if the timing is right.

It's worth noting that the definition of "necessity" may vary among individuals. Some may view it as the bare minimum for survival, while others may consider growth as a necessity. Therefore, it falls upon the leader to clarify this definition and rally support.

Identifying the where and when of change

Change is like a domino effect; one cannot transform an entire organisation instantly but must initiate from a specific point. Once a critical mass is achieved, changes will cascade like dominos toppling one after another. To orchestrate such changes, a leader must identify the first domino to tip and the opportune moment to do so. A harmonious blend of the right place and time is a prerequisite for a leader to instigate change. A mismatch could result in the change losing momentum, facing resistance or hitting a dead-end.

Setting clear and inspiring goals

Human nature is paradoxical – the impossible can either dampen our resolve or fuel our ambition. So, how can leaders motivate change when it seems insurmountable? The answer lies in their ability to kindle hope that the impossible may become possible if clear goals or milestones are achieved. The focus is not so much on the light at the end of the tunnel, but on ensuring everyone believes the tunnel leads to somewhere. In this regard, a leader needs to define clear goals and inspire their achievement to the fullest.

Perseverance: The hallmark of leadership

If there is one quality that distinguishes a visionary leader from a mediocre one, it is perseverance. Perseverance sets apart a leader who can weather the grit of change from one who might not necessarily do a bad job but is simply not the one to lead the change.

Change is challenging. It does not always guarantee success, and it doesn't always go as planned. A leader driving change must be prepared for this, making perseverance an indispensable quality for all change-makers.

Lessons from Cambodia

Cambodia went through a significant transition of leadership when Prime Minister HUN Manet took over from his predecessor, former Prime Minister HUN Sen, known as the "Father of Peace" of Cambodia. His ascent to office marked the beginning of a journey to create a future that Cambodia had only dreamed of. Like other leaders, PM HUN Manet faced many challenges in a world full of uncertainties. He had to deal with resistance to change and decide which traditions to keep and which to let go.

PM HUN Manet used a strategic approach to handle these challenges. He understood that the changes he sought were not just ideas but necessary steps to keep pace with the changing times. After the COVID-19 crisis, with the rise of digital and industrial changes and shifts in global politics, it was clear that Cambodia could not afford to be stagnant. The world was changing, and Cambodia had to change accordingly. PM HUN Manet stepped up as the leader guiding this journey of progress.

The time had also come for Cambodia to shed its image as a war-torn, impoverished nation and envision a brighter future. PM HUN Manet ignited the spark of inspiration, encouraging the nation to look ahead. With its imminent graduation from least developed country (LDC) status, Cambodia aspires to transform into a high-income country by 2050. This ambitious vision necessitated change, and PM HUN Manet stood as the beacon of hope guiding this transformation.

PM HUN Manet answered the question of when and where the changes should start from his first day in office. He believed that change must be driven from within, starting from the highest echelons of government and permeating down to the grassroots. His reforms kicked off from his Prime Minister's Office, extending to his Cabinet ministers, with more transformations on the horizon.

While the goal of achieving the Cambodia Vision 2050 may seem daunting, PM HUN Manet instilled the belief that it is attainable. From graduating the LDC and becoming an upper-middle-income country to building a new labour force capable of leading a 4.0 industrialisation through ambitious programmes such as the 1.5 million youth for TVET (technical and vocational education and training), PM HUN Manet's dream is gradually becoming a reality, garnering the support needed to actualise this change.

PM HUN Manet's perseverance, tested through his academic journey at the United States Military Academy, West Point, and furthered by his education at New York University and Bristol University, now fuels his mission to improve the lives of millions of Cambodians. He remains undeterred, even when faced with obstacles to reforms. His leadership of three national committees on health, education and public service reforms exemplifies his determination to bring about change, despite these issues being among the toughest to tackle. His ability to maintain stability while preserving essential old norms further underscores his leadership prowess. Indeed, PM HUN Manet became the right leader to steer this change, and his capacity to change will undoubtedly usher in a brighter future for Cambodia.

ABOUT PUM HUOT

Pum Huot has been appointed a Member of the Supreme National Economic Council of the Kingdom of Cambodia with the rank of Secretary of State since April 2023. Currently, he holds a position as a Secretary of State at the Office of Council of Ministers, and an Advisor to the Prime Minister of the Kingdom of Cambodia, with ministerial rank. He holds a BA, MA and PhD in Banking, Finance and International Economics.

Leadership Lessons in the Digital Transformation of the Philippine Securities and Exchange Commission

Kelvin Lester K. Lee

It felt like we were under siege.

Looking back on those days when the Company Registration System (CRS) was acting up all the time, I wonder how the Securities and Exchange Commission survived. It was a challenging time, filled with complaints from the public, negative news articles against the Commission, threats of summons (hearings) from the Senate and Congress, and reprimands from the Departments (Ministries) and other higher offices. The CRS was widely condemned. It seemed like everything that had to do with company registration was in chaos. Or at least, it felt like it at that time.

Thankfully, this situation was rectified by the Commission. But it took determined leadership from the Commission En Banc (i.e., the Chairperson and the four Commissioners) and strong support from the different SEC departments and staff to solve this focus. Moreover, it took a clear, focused vision on the part of SEC Chairperson Emilio B. Aquino and his pro-innovation stance to get this done. "I knew where to start – digitally transform the SEC to make business formation and registration easier... to make investors secure in contributing to the growth and success of corporations," Chairperson Aquino once said.

But I may be getting ahead of myself. A quick background may be in order.

The Securities and Exchange Commission of the Philippines

The SEC is the national government regulatory agency charged with supervision over the corporate sector and the capital market. In effect it has a dual mandate. It is both company registrar and securities regulator, making it unique among securities commissions worldwide. Due to this mandate as the company registrar, the SEC is the first step for anyone who wishes to do business in the Philippines, as they would have to register their business entity – typically a corporation – with the Commission first, prior to conducting any form of business in the country.

The Problem: The Company Registration System

In November 2017, the online CRS, which was a software development project contracted to a private sector joint venture, went live. Unfortunately, upon launch, the system almost immediately experienced slowdowns which affected the operating performance of the Commission for company registration.

Incorporations were soon excessively delayed. As a result of the CRS, incorporating a new business in the Philippines could possibly take three months or so rather than the typical three to seven days standard under the old manual paper-based system. Obviously this was quite ironic since the shift to CRS was supposed to speed up the process and make company registration easier and faster.

Although the Commission made many attempts to support the system, including allowing simpler shortcuts in order to enable company registrations to proceed, it was obvious that the problem of delayed registrations wasn't going away. The reality was that there was a problem with the CRS, and we had to come to terms with that. After all, to quote former US President Franklin D. Roosevelt: "Only a foolish optimist can deny the dark realities of the moment."

Leadership Disciplines

That experience of dealing with the CRS problem taught not just myself, but the entire Commission En Banc some valuable leadership disciplines, summed up in what I personally term the Triple Ds:

1. Discuss. A leader must not operate or decide in a vacuum. He must discuss and also gather data and information before making a decision or setting a direction. This can be done through meticulous research, and through discussions or dialogues with experts and stakeholders, among others. In this case, the Commission knew there was a major problem with the CRS. But we needed to better understand the problem, we needed data to

guide us and help us determine what to do, since "it would be best if you did your homework first", as former US Secretary of Defense Jim Mattis shared in his memoir *Call Sign Chaos: Learning to Lead.*

The Commission therefore gathered data and engaged in a series of discussions and dialogues with the private sector, SEC employees and different experts, as well as multilateral organisations and many other stakeholders in order to determine and diagnose the full extent of the problem. One cannot solve a problem if one does not know exactly what the problem is and what is causing it.

Although these dialogues and discussions were often painful, full of recriminations, accusations and finger pointing, they were essential. The SEC had to know and understand the problem. In many of the discussions, even Commissioners like myself at the time had to swallow our pride and accept the often very harsh truth and painful negative feedback thrown at us. I myself was the subject of a furious private reprimand from a minister-level official because of the CRS. I recall other senior SEC officials were likewise admonished in different hearings or meetings too. Overall, it was a painful and humbling experience.

Nevertheless, the feedback from all these discussions proved particularly useful to the Commission as it strived to develop a solution to the failure of the CRS. Through these discussions, we were able to determine the root cause of the issues and how to move on from the problem. The feedback also spurred us to work hard to find a viable solution to the problems.

The Commission soon determined that we couldn't repair or simply patch up the CRS. It became eminently clear that we had to completely replace it, even if it would possibly cause legal and policy problems for the Commission.

The consequences of cancelling a government-procured project like the CRS and of course developing and creating a new system promised to be painful. But at that point, the Commission knew it had to make a decision. A hard one at that.

2. Decide. This particular leadership discipline doesn't get the credit or emphasis it deserves. Decision-making is actually a very challenging and difficult discipline. Some leaders get caught up in decision paralysis, i.e., being unable to make a decision due to too much data or fear of the consequences. I am reminded, however, of what former US President Franklin D. Roosevelt once confided to his staff: "Do the very best in making up your mind, but once your mind is made up go ahead."

In the case of the Commission, it was made abundantly clear that the CRS had to be replaced. We knew there would be risks to us as a Commission – with the guidance of our Chairperson and the shared vision for digital transformation. So we discussed the issues extensively and proceeded to make the difficult decision to remove the CRS and develop a new company registration software to replace it. After all, as Steve Jobs said, "The ability to make tough decisions defines your leadership." This particularly tough decision, in a sense, was to define the Commission for generations to come. As Professor Lim Siong Guan teaches in his book *The Leader, the Teacher & You*: "Leaders must have vision with moral courage and integrity, and conviction to do what is right and not necessarily what is popular." The Commission knew we had to do what was right, with vision, conviction, but most of all, with courage.

Thus, in a series of Commission Meetings, the Commission En Banc then made the pivotal and painful decision to cancel the CRS system. With our decision made, we then set the direction that we would replace it with a different system. These decisions were then incorporated into the SEC Digital Transformation and Technology Modernization Roadmap of the Commission which the Chair and the Commissioners approved. Under this Roadmap the SEC's Information and Communications Technology Department (ICTD) led by its Director Oliver Chato and Assistant Director Archive Navarro were tasked to work on the CRS replacement as soon as possible.

The Commission set strict deadlines for ICTD, in conjunction with the Company Registration and Monitoring Department (CRMD) of the SEC, to develop different software solutions to replace the CRS. In effect, we followed the precept that historian Doris Kearns Goodwin espoused in her book *Leadership in Turbulent Times* in describing the leadership style of FDR, which is to "set a deadline and drive full-bore to meet it".

3. Deliver. With the decision made and a plan of action set and announced, leaders now had to DELIVER on that decision. In this case, the Commission executed and delivered results through its departments. To cut a long, complicated story (and process) short, the Commission's ICTD soon successfully developed the Electronic Simplified Processing of Application for Registration of Companies (eSPARC).

Take note that this particular software was homegrown. Meaning, it was developed completely in-house within the SEC because we were able to hire the best and the brightest through the Chairperson's Hire BnB programme (i.e., Hire the Best and the Brightest). Excellent software programmers and IT leaders had joined the Commission's ICTD at this point and operated under direction we had given them. The eSPARC system, once deployed, was able to incorporate new businesses in only three days or less. The eSPARC was launched in April 2021. This was soon followed in 2022 by the launch of the One Day Submission and E-registration of Companies system (OneSEC), which is a subsystem of the eSPARC system. While eSPARC under its Regular Processing would handle standard company registration applications, which often can be done within a day (up to three days), under OneSEC processing, a company using the standard templates provided by the Commission can be incorporated in a day, sometimes within hours or even minutes.

At the time these were launched and deployed, it caused a sensation in the Philippine legal and business landscape. Many businessmen and lawyers couldn't believe how fast and painless the eSPARC and the OneSEC were. One prominent example was the incorporation of a non-stock corporation using OneSEC which was incorporated in only around 15 minutes, with no less than the President of the Philippines as witness.

It was, literally, a Digital Transformation.

The Commission and its leadership received multiple accolades because of the delivery and deployment of these systems. In 2023, the SEC won the Corporate Registers Forum Innovation Award for eSPARC and OneSEC in Malta. In that same year, the SEC set a new record high of 46,000 successfully registered corporations. The SEC also received the Excellence in Digital Transformation Award during the GCash Digital Excellence Awards. Chairperson Aquino, the Chief Architect of the SEC's Digital Transformation Roadmap, was named the first ever Public Sector Innovator in the Mansmith Innovation Awards, and IDC CEO of the year, among many other awards, while I had the honour to be recognised as a Digital Leader during the Spark Digital Leaders Award.

This brings to mind what Arnold Schwarzenegger once wrote in his book, *Be Useful*, quoting American country singer Jimmy Dean, he said: "Do what you say you're going to do, and try to do it a little better than you said you would." In this case, I believe that the Commission has done <u>more</u> than what it said it would do and <u>better</u> than what it set out to do. The SEC delivered.

Conclusion

The experience of undergoing the digital transformation of the SEC in particular its Company Registration system, was certainly challenging. But the Commission En Banc more than met that challenge, as can be seen in this particular success story. But I must emphasise the point: This would not have been possible without strong, visionary and decisive leadership embodied by the leadership disciplines discussed in this essay.

Discuss, Decide and Deliver – all these disciplines combine to form a fundamental pathway to successful leadership. Leadership in this case meant having the strength of will and moral conviction to move forward with what needed to be done. This was of course done in a data-driven and technical manner, but at the end of the day, it takes courage and commitment to move forward to make a decision for the good of the country (even if it is possibly to your own detriment) and then delivering on that decision.

Although I am no longer a Commissioner as of this writing (my tenure ended in March 2024), I will be forever proud that I was once one of the Commissioners who, alongside our Chairperson and his direction, made the decision and delivered on the Commission's Digital Transformation. It was an honour to serve. And I am happy that when it comes to business registrations in the Philippines, it is now – to quote one of Chairperson Aquino's favorite sayings – "Easy at SEC."

ABOUT KELVIN LESTER K. LEE

Atty. Kelvin Lester K. Lee is a Senior Financial Sector Specialist of an international development organisation. He previously served as a Commissioner of the Securities and Exchange Commission of the Philippines (SEC) and as Assistant Secretary at the Office of the President of the Philippines. He was a Lee Kuan Yew Senior Fellow in Public Service of the National University of Singapore (2022).

Chek Jawa[1]

Tan Yong Soon

Singapore is a small island city-state. Even with a Government policy of active land reclamation, which has added to its total land area by more than 20% from the 1960s, Singapore remains land scarce. Hence there is a need for long-term integrated planning to cater for economic growth and a good quality of life, maintain a clean and green environment, and make the best use of its land resources.

The Urban Redevelopment Authority (URA) is the government agency entrusted with the long-term integrated planning. The URA does this through the Concept Plan (now called the Long-Term Plan) and the Master Plan. The Concept Plan is reviewed every 10 years or so. The Concept Plan rethinks what Singapore can look like in the next 50 years and beyond.

---

[1] The essay "Chek Jawa" by Prof Tan Yong Soon first appeared in *Peace with Nature: 50 Inspiring Essays on Nature and the Environment*, edited by Tommy Koh, Lye Lin Heng and Shawn Lum, published by World Scientific in 2023.

The Master Plan is reviewed every five years and translates the broad strategies of the Concept Plan into detailed plans to guide the development of land and property. It is the statutory land use plan that shows the permissible land use and density for developments in Singapore.

When I was posted to the URA as its CEO in June 2001, the work on the Concept Plan 2001 had just been completed. It had started in 1998, with the public consultation exercise commencing from August 2000 following the formation of focus groups. A public forum was organised in December 2000. Feedback from the entire engagement exercise was incorporated into the draft Concept Plan that was exhibited from 28 April to 11 May 2001. A final public dialogue was held on 11 May 2001 to gather feedback on the draft plan before the release of the final plan in July 2001. My focus was to review the proposals in the Concept Plan and to subsequently incorporate them into the Master Plan 2003.

The presence of marine life in the Chek Jawa inter-tidal zone was first raised during the final public forum on 11 May 2001 by Joseph Lai, who had stumbled upon it recently. A newspaper feature article was published on 8 July 2001. It carried comments by Chua Sek Chuan and Shawn Lum, chairman of the Marine Conservation group and the Plant group respectively, of the Nature Society, on the beauty and the significance of the new discovery. The public started to visit the place and letters, including one from Geh Min, President of the Nature Society, were published in *The Straits Times* Forum Page to urge the preservation of Chek Jawa.

Reclamation of Chek Jawa had been decided as early as 1992 and mentioned in the Master Plan 1998. Detailed preparations were already underway. A study commissioned by the Housing and Development Board (HDB), the agency that was in charge of the reclamation works, had found that the reclamation would not have significant impact on the dugong population (an endangered mammal that mainly subsists on seagrass), because the seagrass in Chek Jawa was found to be patchy; moreover, there did not appear to be a resident dugong population there. The National Parks Board (NParks) had surveyed the area around Chek Jawa and found it did not have established coral reefs or reef communities; it would transplant the affected plants to other parts of the island. The URA thus put out a public reply in July 2001 to explain the need for the reclaimed land, the actions taken and that the reclamation would proceed as planned in December 2001.

The inter-tidal marine life was missed by government agencies and the Nature Society (Singapore), experts and laymen, until it was stumbled upon in December 2000. Would the new discovery at this late stage merit a re-thinking of the planned reclamation? As a public servant, my job is to improve the quality of living of Singaporeans and their future generations. I strongly believe in the importance and priorities of security and economic development, having spent much of my career in the Ministries of Defence and Finance. But both security and economic development are means to an end. The end is a better quality of living and sustainable development for Singapore and Singaporeans. Decision-making must be evidence-based.

Intellectual humility, the willingness to be open to learn from others, to listen, and to seek clarity is important. And should significant facts change, there must be courage to change the decision.

Behind closed doors and away from public eyes, I signalled to my staff a willingness to review the matter. The URA staff was to carefully study the evidence received from experts, members of the public and the Nature Society (Singapore), which sent in files with photographs of what they had found in 2001. The URA would then study the merits of keeping the place and the implications of proceeding with or calling off the planned reclamation.

New studies of the marine life in the Chek Jawa inter-tidal zone made available to the URA did reveal the rich and unique biodiversity value of the area. URA planners studied many options, including different reclamation profiles and their implications on land use and environmental impacts. Could the reclamation be modified so that we could preserve the marine life and also have land for our use? URA officers involved include my deputy and Chief Planner Koh Wen Gin, key people in the Physical Planning division such as Michael Koh, Lim Eng Hwee and Hwang Yu-ning, as well as younger planners such as Lim Swee Keng and Mieko Otsuki. They were conscientious, curious, and creative. They weighed the implications and worked at various options. The matter was urgent as the reclamation contract had already been awarded and preparatory work had begun. The URA put up papers at the Ministry of National Development (MND)'s HQ meetings, and briefing and discussion sessions were held with Minister for National Development, Mah Bow Tan.

I invited Minister Mah to visit Chek Jawa during a low tide to see the place for himself. He accepted and the date was fixed on 18 October 2001. On that day, my key planning staff and I gathered at Changi Point, together with the NParks Chairman Leo Tan and the NParks CEO Tan Wee Kiat. We were met by Loh Yan Hui from the HDB, the project director of the proposed reclamation.

While waiting for the Minister and the Permanent Secretary, we heard on radio that Parliament was to be prorogued. Despite the fact that General Elections would be held soon (it was later set for 3 November), Minister Mah turned up. Chek Jawa was clearly an important issue close to his heart. We took the boat to Pulau Ubin. On site, NParks officers briefed us on the flora and fauna and the ecosystems in Chek Jawa, while HDB officers briefed us on the impending reclamation works. We walked along the shore and saw rich marine life – anemones, sea stars, sponges, horseshoe crabs and others. We witnessed the joys and excitement of Singaporean families and friends, including young children, having fun trekking on the shores, discovering and examining various sea species. There was a sizeable crowd. The Minister spoke with a number of them and spent three hours on the ground to obtain a good appreciation of the area.

On the way back to Changi, we all felt Chek Jawa would be worth preserving. Back in the office, URA officers worked frenetically to finalise the report. Expert views from the NUS Department of Biological Sciences, Tropical Marine Science

Institute and Raffles Museum of Biodiversity Research, as well as detailed reports from the Nature Society (Singapore) and other interested parties were taken into consideration. Revised land reclamation profile options, costs and implications were re-examined. The conclusion was that reclamation, if carried out, would have to be limited to a very small area so as not to harm the fragile ecosystem. However, reclaiming such a small area would not be cost-effective. Coordination was conducted with various government agencies to seek and finalise strategic viewpoints as not proceeding with the planned reclamation would have important implications.

The Government agreed to put off the land reclamation works and retain Chek Jawa in its pristine state for the continued enjoyment of all. The decision had the caveat, "for as long as the Pulau Ubin island is not needed for development". Minister Mah met with interested parties and experts before the official announcement was made on 14 January 2002. Chek Jawa, a unique natural area and one of Singapore's richest ecosystems, was thus saved for the enjoyment of Singaporeans and visitors. It was placed under the management of NParks.

Everyone – the public, nature lovers, public agencies and the Government – contributed to this good outcome. Members of the public – especially the Nature Society (Singapore)'s marine conservation section – provided new information on the area's biodiversity, information that was insightful and detailed. The feedback was reasoned and not confrontational. The Government and its agencies were open to feedback, gathered additional expert views and took a pragmatic approach. The URA's planning process was rigorous, and yet URA planners were open to look at new information and had the courage to review its long established position. The Government took the long view and endorsed sustainable development and was willing to reverse its decision.

The Chek Jawa decision is an example of clarity and courage in decision-making. It is not so much a turning point in government policy as it is a good model of public consultation at work. It was made possible because the public and government agencies had collaborated positively and responsibly.

The civil service was keen to learn from the episode and the URA collaborated with the Civil Service College to write a case on Chek Jawa for teaching purposes in its senior programmes.

Singapore will always have to balance development with nature. Not every issue can be resolved to the satisfaction of all parties. But working together, with a culture of collaboration and caringness – care for the community beyond our immediate family, care for both people and nature, and care for the long term and future generations – we will all be able to unlearn, reinvent and achieve for the good of Singapore.

ABOUT TAN YONG SOON

Tan Yong Soon is a former senior civil servant who served as Permanent Secretary in the Ministry of the Environment and Water Resources, and for Climate Change in the Prime Minister's Office; Chief Executive Officer of the Urban Redevelopment Authority, Deputy Secretary in the Ministry of Finance and the Ministry of Defence, and Principal Private Secretary to the Prime Minister. He is Professor in Practice at the Lee Kuan Yew School of Public Policy, National University of Singapore, where he started the LKY Senior Fellows in Public Service Programme. He co-authored the book, *Clean, Green and Blue: Singapore's Journey Towards Environmental and Water Sustainability* (Singapore: ISEAS, 2008) and edited the book, *50 Years of Environment*, as part of the World Scientific series on Singapore's 50 Years of Nation Building.

PART

HOW TO BECOME
A LEADER

Y ou know what a leader does – the V.I.P. functions.
You know what you need to do – the 5Cs.
You know the importance of Character.
But to become a leader, you need to know:

- How to manage yourself

- How to manage your boss and build relationships

- How to manage luck

Part 3 of this book has three chapters, and ends with five essays. The essay by Ahmaddin Abdul Rahman, Minister of Home Affairs, Brunei, focuses on "The Essence of Leadership". Hong Hai, Nanyang Technological University Emeritus Professor, writes on the importance of being First Class. Trained in engineering, management and economics, he has worked in public service, the private sector and academia. Cham Tao Soon, the inaugural President of Nanyang Technology University for 21 years from 1981 to 2002, writes about "Education in the Era of Disruptive Technology". I share my speech as Guest of Honour at the 184th Raffles Institution Founder's Day in 2007, in which I spoke about leadership and the environment. To round off this section is the essay "Nurturing Tomorrow's Leaders" by Professor Tan Eng Chye, President of the National University of Singapore.

CHAPTER 12

Managing Oneself

A
n oracle is someone who has the power of foresight and can give wise and insightful advice or prophetic predictions.

In ancient Greece, the oracle communicates divine knowledge from God to mortal, known as divination, which played an important role in Greek religion. The most famous and powerful oracle is the priestess of Apollo, otherwise known as the Pythia and Oracle of Delphi, who provided divine advice from Apollo. Apollo is well-known as the Greek god of prophecy, with the ability to see into the future. The ruins of the Temple of Apollo at Delphi still stand today and is recognised by the United Nations Educational, Scientific and Cultural Organization (UNESCO) as a World Heritage Site, having had a great influence in the ancient world.

The Oracle's divinatory power is never in question, although it can be subject to misinterpretation. Croesus, the incredibly wealthy king of Lydia, had asked the Oracle if he would be successful in a war campaign against Persia. The Oracle replied that Croesus would "destroy a great empire". Croesus, mistaken that he would defeat the Persians, launched the attack and was captured instead. The story of Croesus is one of human failing and not knowing himself and the enemy.

There are some 150 maxims inscribed in and around the temple, including Nothing in Excess, Follow God, Obey the Law, Respect Your Parents.

The best-known maxim is "Know Thyself", inscribed prominently at the entrance to the temple.

Know Thyself

This is wisdom since ancient times in all civilisations.

Sun Tzu, in *The Art of War,* tells us to know yourself and the enemy: "If you know the enemy and know yourself, you need not fear the result of a hundred battles. If you know yourself but not the enemy, for every victory gained you will also suffer a defeat. If you know neither the enemy nor yourself, you will succumb in every battle" (as translated by Lionel Giles).

Peter Drucker, in his seminal work, "Managing Oneself" (*Harvard Business Review,* 1999), wrote, "To succeed at work, we need to know ourselves." We need to know:

- our strengths
- how do we perform
- our values
- where we belong
- what should we contribute

A person can only perform from strength. One cannot perform on weaknesses, let alone on something one cannot do at all. It is useful to be reminded that performing from strengths doesn't mean we ignore our weaknesses or our bias, or prejudice.

So, you will have to:

1. concentrate on your strengths

2. work on improving your strengths

3. work on acquiring skills and knowledge you need to fully realise your strengths, i.e., "disabling ignorance"

4. remedy your bad habits

How do I perform? According to Drucker, how one performs is individual. It is personality. It is a given. It can be modified, but is unlikely to be changed. "Do not try to change yourself – it is unlikely to be successful. But work, and hard, to improve the way you perform."

What are my values? "To be effective in an organisation, one's own values must be compatible with the organisation's values. They need not be the same. But they must be close enough so that they can co-exist. Otherwise, the person will be frustrated, but also the person will not produce results," Drucker advised.

But even if the person produces results, values are and should be the ultimate test. "There rarely is a conflict between a person's strengths and the way the person performs. There is sometimes a conflict between a person's values and the person's strengths. What one does well – even very well – and successfully may not fit with one's value system. It may not appear to that person as making a contribution and as something to which to devote one's life."

Where do I belong? The answers to the three questions: "What are my strengths? How do I perform? What are my values?" should enable the individual to decide where he or she belongs.

This is not a decision that most people can or should make at the beginning of their careers. But at some point, they can and should decide where they do belong, or rather where they do not belong. Drucker wrote that "knowing the answers to these three questions enables people to say no to an opportunity, to an offer, to an assignment, 'Yes, I'll do that. But this is the way I should be doing it. This is the way it should be structured. This is the way my relationships should be. These are the results you should expect from me and in this time frame, because this is who I am.'" Of course, not every person can say no or negotiate the terms with the boss. You could only do so if you have a good track record, built up a strong emotional bank account and when there is trust in the relationship.

According to Drucker, successful careers are not planned. They are the careers of people who are prepared for the opportunity because they know their strengths, the way they work and their values. For knowing where one belongs makes ordinary people – hardworking, competent but mediocre otherwise – into outstanding performers.

We should develop and improve ourselves, and position ourselves where we should contribute. But where should we contribute?

Here, Drucker advised that the decision "What should my contributions be?" balances three elements:

- What does the situation require?
- How could I make the greatest contributions with my strengths, my way of performing, my values, to what needs to be done?
- What results must be achieved to make a difference? (The results should be: hard to achieve, but achievable; meaningful; able to make a difference; visible and, if possible, measurable.)

Know Our Bias

We must also be conscious of our bias. We use unconscious routines, known as heuristics, to cope with the complexity inherent in most decisions. But heuristics are not foolproof, resulting in flaws in the way we think in making decisions. Because they are hardwired into our thinking process, we fail to recognise them. There are many types of heuristics. The most common are availability, representatives and anchoring-and-adjustment.

Daniel Kahneman described these and other biases in *Thinking, Fast and Slow* (2011). He wrote about the two systems of thinking as follows:

- System 1 thinking or <u>Fast Thinking</u>. Operates automatically and quickly. The intuitive reactions and quick judgments that we rely on for most decisions are also the process that leads to far greater biases in judgment.

- System 2 thinking or <u>Slow Thinking</u>. Effortful. We allocate attention to the effortful activities. Our more deliberative thought processes can be used to dampen the negative effects of our intuitive judgments.

Kahneman also warned us against WYSIATI (What You See Is All There Is). WYSIATI means that we use the information we have as if it is the only information. We don't spend much time saying, "Well, there is much we don't know." We make do with what we do know. And that concept is very central to the functioning of our mind.

WYSIATI is the failure to realise how little info there is, or not wanting more info to spoil the story. According to Kahneman, "Our comforting conviction that the world makes sense rests on our secure foundation: <u>our unlimited ability to ignore our ignorance.</u>"

In managing ourselves, leaders must avoid the illusion of control and over-confidence, and should (be wise to) know:

- What do we know (and not know)? What are our biases?
- Who, where and how do we ask? Who and what do we trust?
- How do we decide? What are the consequences?

Take George Shultz, an outstanding public service leader who served as Ronald Reagan's Secretary of State at the end of the Cold War, and before that he was Secretary of Treasury and Secretary of Labor under Richard Nixon. Schultz was an extremely wise and experienced man. In 2011, at age 90 and with no biomedical expertise, he joined the Theranos Board of Directors, and later helped recruit Henry Kissinger and other top political figures to the Board. He also encouraged his grandson to join Theranos upon his graduation in 2013. When the grandson raised concerns about Theranos, Schultz dismissed the concerns, telling his grandson, "I'm over 90 years old. I've seen a lot in my time, and I've been right almost every time and I know I'm right about this." (*Guardian*, 10 January 2023) Theranos, a health technology company, was subsequently shut down by the US Securities and Exchange Commission in 2018.

The best defence against over-confidence is awareness and humility.

Power and Influence

Why should people listen or follow you? The concepts of power and leadership are interconnected. An individual cannot be a leader without having power. Power and influence are critical for effective leadership and managerial behaviour. It is important that the leader understands how to exercise power and influence to get things done <u>through</u> others.

Social psychologists John French and Bertram Raven (*The Bases of Social Power*, 1959) identified six bases of power as follows:

1. Legitimate Power

2. Reward Power

3. Coercive Power

4. Information Power (this was added later in 1965)

5. Expert Power

6. Referent Power
   a. Relationships
   b. Charisma

The bases of power can be grouped into two kinds of power: positional and personal power. Of the six bases listed above, the first four come from positional power, the latter two from personal power.

The leader must have both positional and personal power. He is a leader not merely because of his position in the organisation. He must demonstrate a level of skill, competence and experience that achieve results and help make him trustworthy. He must develop relations and connections and earn the respect and trust of his followers.

Good leaders understand the power of relationships. People with positional power need to exhibit personal power to effectively influence all working under them. They need to develop their leadership skills to maintain the power vested in them by the organisation.

Whether or not we aspire leadership positions, we need to appreciate that leadership is part of everyday life. We are all leaders (and followers) at all levels. We must first manage ourselves before we can lead others.

References

Drucker, Peter, "Managing Oneself", *Harvard Business Review*, January 2005.

Kahneman, Daniel, *Thinking, Fast and Slow*. NY: Farrar, Straus & Giroux Inc, 2011.

CHAPTER 13

Managing Your Boss and Building Relationships

To manage oneself requires taking relationship responsibility. Peter Drucker pointed out that this means:

1. <u>Accept that other people are as much individuals as one is oneself.</u> To be effective, one therefore must know the strengths, the performance modes and the values of people one works with – especially the bosses. And it is incumbent on the people who work with them "to observe them, to find out how they work and to adapt themselves to the way the bosses are effective".

2. <u>To take responsibility for communications.</u> We should ask ourselves: Who needs to know about our strengths, how we perform, etc. – it is the people whom we depend on and people who depend on us – our superiors, colleagues, team members, subordinates. It is advisable to communicate our expectations to them. Doing so helps build understanding and trust.

Managing Our Boss

Among the work relationships, the relationship with the boss is perhaps the most important. What is the manager-boss relationship like and how do we manage our boss?

Some people behave as if their bosses are not very dependent on them. Some people see themselves as not very dependent on their bosses. Many managers assume that their boss will magically know what information or help their subordinates need and provide them.

The truth is one that recognises the mutual dependence of the participants. According to John Gabarro and John Kotter (Managing Your Boss, *Harvard Business Review*, January 2005), "bosses need cooperation, reliability and honesty from their direct reports. Managers, for their part, rely on bosses for making connections with the rest of the company, for setting priorities, and for obtaining critical resources."

Our boss is not omniscient or omnipotent. He is fallible and imperfect. He has deadlines, worries, anxieties. He needs our help and cooperation to do his job effectively. We need to appreciate his goals, his pressures, and help him to achieve his objectives.

Gabarro and Kotter wrote that "managing your boss requires that you gain an understanding of the boss and his or her context, as well as your own situation. All managers do this to some degree, but many are not thorough enough."

The subordinate needs to understand what his boss' expectations are and maintain a relationship based on mutual expectations.

What is the boss's work style? For instance, in terms of information, does he want more or less? Early or late? Verbal or written? To hear good news only? We need to understand his work style and maintain a relationship that fits both your needs and styles. It is key to develop trust and a relationship based on dependability and honesty.

Understand that the boss is also limited in his time, resources and influence (probably as much as us) and the subordinate should make selective use of his time and resources, e.g., in resolving turf issues with another department.

"Although a superior-subordinate relationship is one of mutual dependence, it is also one in which the subordinate is typically more dependent on the boss than the other way around.

"This dependence inevitably results in the subordinate feeling a certain degree of frustration, sometimes anger, when his actions or options are constrained by his boss's decisions.

"The way in which a manager handles these frustrations largely depends on his or her predisposition toward dependence on authority figures."

According to Gabarro and Kotter:

- A counter-dependent manager sees the boss as someone who, by virtue of the role, is a hindrance to progress, an obstacle to be circumvented or at best tolerated. When such a manager acts on his negative feelings, often in subtle and non-verbal ways, the boss sometimes does become the enemy.

- An over-dependent manager sees the boss as if he were an all-wise parent who should know best, should take responsibility for their careers, train them in all they need to know and protect them from overly ambitious peers.

Gabarro and Kotter advised that "an awareness of these extremes and the range between them can be very useful in understanding where your own predispositions fall and what the implications are for how you tend to behave in relation to your boss.

"If you believe, on the one hand, that you have some tendencies toward counter-dependence, you can understand and even predict what your reactions and overreactions are likely to be.

"If, on the other hand, you believe you have some tendencies toward overdependence, you might question the extent to which your overcompliance or inability to confront real differences may be making both you and your boss less effective."

Mutual expectations

Gabarro and Kotter wrote that "the subordinate who passively assumes that he or she knows what the boss expects is in for trouble. Of course, some superiors will spell out their expectations very explicitly and in great detail. But most do not. And although many corporations have systems that provide a basis for communicating expectations (such as performance appraisal reviews), these systems never work perfectly. Also, between these formal reviews, expectations invariably change. Ultimately, the burden falls on the subordinate to find out what the boss's expectations are."

Flow of information

According to Gabarro and Kotter, "How much information a boss needs about what a subordinate is doing will vary significantly depending on the boss's style, the situation he is in, and the confidence the boss has in the subordinate. But it is not uncommon for a boss to need more information than the subordinate would naturally supply or for the subordinate to think the boss knows more than he or she really does. Effective managers recognise that they probably underestimate what their bosses need to know and make sure they find ways to keep them informed through processes that fit their styles.

"Managing the flow of information upward is particularly difficult if the boss does not like to hear about problems. Nevertheless, for the good of the organisation, the boss, and the subordinate, a superior needs to hear about failures as well as successes."

Gabarro and Kotter further caution that "no doubt, some subordinates will resent that on top of all their other duties, they also need to take time and energy to manage their relationships with their bosses. Such managers fail to realise the importance of this activity and how it can simplify their jobs by eliminating potentially severe problems. Effective managers recognise that this part of their work is legitimate. Seeing themselves as ultimately responsible for what they achieve in an organisation, they know they need to establish and manage relationships with everyone on whom they depend – and that includes the boss."

You need to develop and maintain a relationship that:

- fits both your needs and styles
- is characterised by mutual expectations
- keeps your boss informed
- is based on dependability and honesty
- selectively uses your boss's time and resources

Peers and Subordinates

In addition to our work relationship with the boss, the work relationship with our peers and subordinates is also important. Especially in the public service, we need whole-of-government coordination and networked governance. Working well with peers across various agencies is required.

Beyond our work colleagues, we need to maintain ties with friends. Mark Granovetter in his article "The Strength of Weak Ties" (*American Journal of Sociology* Vol. 78, No. 6 [1973]), theorised that weak ties (think casual acquaintances, friends-of-friends and other arm's-length relationships) help disseminate new information and provide more job opportunities than strong ties (such as close friends, family or immediate co-workers).

The power of weak ties in gaining new employment is validated in a recent experiment co-led by researchers from Stanford, Massachusetts Institute of Technology, Harvard and LinkedIn ("A Causal Test of the Strength of Weak Ties", *Science,* September 2022), using data from 20 million LinkedIn profiles over five years that shows how much we rely on people we know less well to land new jobs.

The researchers found that in terms of interaction intensity (based on the number of messaging interactions people had), the weakest ties produce the most results, and the strongest ties produce the least job transmission. But in structural terms (based on the number of mutual friends two users had in common), moderately weak ties are the best – not the weakest, but slightly stronger than the weakest. The inflection point is around 10 mutual connections between people; if you share more than that with someone on LinkedIn, the usefulness of your connection to the other person, in job-hunting terms, diminishes. Also, the usefulness of weak ties varies by industry on LinkedIn. The power of weak ties on the site is especially strong in high-tech industries.

References

Kotter, John P., and Gabarro, John, J. "Managing Your Boss", *Harvard Business Review*, January 2005.

CHAPTER 14

Managing Luck

Daniel Kahneman is known to cite the following as his favourite equation:

Success = talent + luck
Great success = a little more talent + a lot of luck

Kahneman's implication in his book *Thinking, Fast and Slow* (2011) is that the difference between moderate and great success is mostly luck, not talent or skill. Chance plays a much greater role in our careers than we might wish or even realise.

Morten Hansen (UC Berkeley) tells us "You Can Manage Luck. Here's How" (*Harvard Business Review*, 4 November 2011). Hansen and Jim Collins, co-authors of *Great by Choice* (Random House, 2011) analysed the history of luck events for the companies in their study set and found that "winners and average performers encountered essentially the same number of luck and unlucky events. It is not the luck you get that counts; it is what you do with it – your return on luck."

How can you get a high return on luck at work?

1. View life as a flow of luck events. When you start having this "luck flow" mindset, you can start managing those events to your advantage, but only then.

2. Prepare for bad-luck events (they will come). The best leaders in their study prepared for bad-luck events by building reserves and running lean operations in good times. Likewise, we can prepare by incorporating safety margins, acquiring options and building a strong network of people who can help.

3. Spot good-luck events when they come. When confronted with a luck event, small or large, take a moment to zoom out ("what are we trying to accomplish here?"), then zoom in (get the details right).

4. Execute brilliantly on good-luck events. You must prepare intensively, commit all the resources you can and be maniacal about execution when good-luck moments arrive.

"Luck is what happens when preparation meets opportunity."

This quote, attributed to Roman philosopher Seneca, reminds us that we make our own luck.

So how do we make our own luck?

If we view life as a flow of luck events, we need to find the fast flow – get to be where things are happening and surround ourselves with a lot of people and interaction. We need to meet people. People make things happen. It is not necessarily friends, just contacts. But we also need to let people know what we are trying to do or where we want to go. We need to show people we are capable and helpful.

Tommy Koh and UNCLOS III

Tommy Koh was President of the Third United Nations Convention on the Law of the Sea (UNCLOS) 1980-82 and is widely respected for getting the Convention passed.

UNCLOS III was convened in 1973 and concluded in 1982 after nine years of negotiations and working through a complex agenda covering over 25 subjects and issues. These ranged from the exploration and exploitation of the international area, straits used for international navigation, exclusive economic zones, landlocked and geographically disadvantaged states, to the protection of the marine environment and marine scientific research. UNCLOS is extremely important to the world and especially crucial for Singapore, given that our overall trade is more than three times our GDP, and much of our trade is carried over the seas. So how did Tommy Koh, a young representative of a small and young nation, get to become the President of the Convention?

Tommy Koh (Singapore's Permanent Representative to the United Nations, New York 1968-71 and 1974-84) was involved in UNCLOS III from the start of its formal negotiations in 1974. He worked hard and made himself useful. He was the chairman of a key negotiation committee that dealt with the financial arrangements for seabed mining in UNCLOS III in 1978, and was described in a *The New Yorker* magazine article as "one of the most often consulted and most hardworking men at the conference; some delegates considered him its most brilliant member.... The major issues in these negotiations, which had once inflamed the Seventy-seven and the mining corporations equally, had simmered down since Koh took over."

In December 1980, the universally popular President of the Conference, Hamilton Shirley Amerasinghe (Sri Lanka), suffered a stroke and died. There was no agreement on a successor among the major camps. Tommy was the consensus candidate, was elected in March 1981 as the President and chaired the negotiations to a successful closure in 1982.

Tommy Koh went on to chair the United Nations' hugely important 1992 Rio Earth Summit (officially known as the United Nations

Conference on Environment and Development), which, when it was held, was the largest ever gathering of world leaders. Treaties and documents signed at the Earth Summit helped build a global consensus for the first time on pursuing economic growth in ways that protected the environment – covering everything from biodiversity to greenhouse gas emissions.

Tommy Koh went on to take on many assignments, both nationally and internationally. Among his international awards are the Champion of the Earth by the United Nations Environment Programme in 2006 and the Great Negotiator Award by the Program on Negotiation at Harvard Law School in 2014.

Tommy Koh's example serves to illustrate the following points raised earlier:

- surround ourselves with a lot of people and interaction (beyond working hard, making ourselves useful)
- meet people to make things happen, reach out, build networks
- show people we are capable and helpful, e.g., willingness to step up when no one else was willing

Best of luck!

Reference

Hansen, Morten, "You Can Manage Luck. Here's How", *Harvard Business Review*, 4 November 2011.

The Essence of Leadership

Ahmaddin Abdul Rahman

Leadership is a topic of paramount importance, a quality that has a profound impact on organisations, communities and societies globally. Leadership is not confined to a particular title or position. In today's ever so rapidly evolving world, effective leadership is cultivated and practised to navigate the challenges and opportunities that arise. Success is only achieved when leaders inspire, foster collaboration and have a shared *raison d'etre* with proper guidance. A good leader harnesses an untapped potential in the hope that the shared intelligence and creativity will create a trickling down effect to community. I believe that the true essence of leadership lies in the ability to put ourselves in another person's shoe, with the right intention to help and to change for the greater good of the community.

All throughout the years where I have been placed in a position of leadership, I have been exposed to handling domestic challenges using the top-down approach. This has been a practised and proven efficiency as I have served the Government of Brunei since 1997 for 27 years. In the time of my leadership, it was emphasised for leaders to be aware and up to date on the hidden unheard struggles of the community. It was only with this top-down approach were the difficulties of the communities unveiled and solved. One of the ways an organisation can impose the top-down approach is by having forums with marginalised groups of the community as a way to show commitment in taking care of their needs and welfare. On that note, as a leader gains more exposure with the community, the community will gain more trust in the capabilities of the leader in improving the status quo.

One would question if the best leadership style lies in the leader's priority in giving confidence or motivation to their organisation and society. However, I believe confidence and motivation go hand in hand. The role of a leader is to inspire a clear-cut vision of the future that pushes others to join them and achieve that shared aspiration. Leaders should be honest and transparent in creating goals and vision in their organisations. The values of leadership know no title and no social positions in society. Within diverse communities and nations, leadership plays a crucial role in promoting social cohesion and advancing collective well-being. Leaders must be eager and committed to lifelong learning amongst diverse individuals and communities. Inspirational leaders ignite hope, and are a catalyst for transformative change, leaving a permanent positive mark on organisations and communities.

Leaders carry the burden of shaping the next generation of leaders' working styles and work flows as a torch of progress in the near future. It is about embracing innovation, adaptation and forward-thinking strategies to address the uncertainties and challenges of our time. The hallmark of efficient leadership is one that must be willing to embrace different leadership styles and adjust their mindsets to changing circumstances. Leaders should welcome with open arms to new innovations, and advanced technologies and systems in order to stay on course towards the consensus goal.

A leader must be inclusive and cooperative. This enables quick innovative solutions, ease in sharing resources and a common ground in making concessions for the greater good. Compromise means finding ways to balance competing interests and methods rather than sacrificing principles, not only within their own organisations but also external sectors/parties in both national and international spheres. However, with such responsibility, a leader must ensure that all segments of society are represented, heard and seen. Such an approach allows growth in the qualities of exceptional leaders, fostering inclusivity, and encourages open-minded thinking and efficient decision-making.

Effective leaders invest in the growth and development of their team members. Giving recognition to the strengths of their team members, leaders inspire; giving confidence and motivation which enables individuals to reach their potential to the very fullest. However, although it is important to give credit to their broad-thinking, a leader must still communicate their vision, expectations and feedback as transparently as possible with only the intention to improve and solve problems efficiently. This in turn will help leaders set the tone for behaviour and performance expected through their own actions, allowing team members to learn the leader's thinking and build rapport with each other. With this value of a true leader, this will exercise empathy, humility and decisiveness in further developing a quality leader.

Ultimately, being a leader means that one must internalise the challenges they face through experience. One of the greatest challenges a leader may face would be confronting changing environments in terms of people and place. Over the course of a leader's life, one must understand how important it is to have strength and integrity.

In essence, a visionary leader that embraces diversity fosters a culture of innovation, empowerment and high performance, enhancing productivity and fostering employee engagement with a sense of purpose and belonging. Visionary leaders aim to align individual aspirations with organisational goals, unlocking the full potential of their teams and eventually nurturing a competent successor. Leaders not only have the privilege to be role models in values, behaviours and leadership qualities for the greater good, but they also carry great responsibility in maintaining and upholding the high standards, authenticity, support and guidance throughout their term. With great leadership, comes greater responsibilities.

"If you are afraid,
Then you are not sincere"
Ahmaddin Abdul Rahman

ABOUT AHMADDIN ABDUL RAHMAN

Dato Haji Ahmaddin has been the Minister of Home Affairs, Brunei, since 7 June 2022. He previously held the posts of Deputy Minister of Finance and Economy (Fiscal); Permanent Secretary (Policy and Investment); and Permanent Secretary (Corporate and Performance) in the Ministry of Finance and Economy. His passion for information technology, combined with a focus on enforcement, has led to the implementation of key initiatives. Some of these enterprises include the E-Payment Gateway for the Treasury Department, and National Welfare System which consolidates the Welfare System Application with various governmental agencies. The Immigration National Registration System and National Labour Management System are his current projects to strengthen the process of hiring foreign labour as well as streamline the process of visa applications and passes.

The Importance of
Being First Class[1]

Hong Hai

"Being comfortable in our own skins is an important part of one's individual resilience."

Friday 13 May 1969. It seemed an evening just like any other in Kuala Lumpur. I was ready to head downtown to spend an evening out with the boys when the phone rang. It was one of the friends I was to meet in town. I can still vividly recall his words.

"Don't leave your house. Go turn on the news."

The television news announced the imposition of a curfew. Had the phone call come a minute later, I would have already left the house. I cannot imagine what might have happened to me, as I would have driven along the Federal Highway from

---

[1]   The essay "The Importance of Being First Class" by Dr Hong Hai first appeared in *Profiles in Resilience: Reflections in the Time of Covid-19*, edited by Kua Ee Heok and Abdullah Tarmugi, published by Write Editions in 2021.

Petaling Jaya to Kuala Lumpur. Along the highway violence had broken out and many innocent Chinese were slaughtered, including a friend of mine who was in a car with his Malay girlfriend.

That evening saw the grisly beginning of the worst racial riot in Malaysian history. Racial tension had been rising, fanned by the inflammatory rhetoric of Malay leaders angry over their losses in the recent general election. Emotions were also raised by the exuberant jubilation displayed in street parades by non-Malay voters. I was to learn much later from political analysts that the riots may not have been simply the spontaneous result of heated feelings over the election. There have been unconfirmed rumours that there was a plot to oust popular Prime Minister Tengku Abdul Rahman. The Tengku was indeed sidelined after May 13, and later stepped down.

It changed inexorably the course of Malaysian history.

For about two weeks after that night, my three bachelor housemates and I were under curfew and were virtually imprisoned in a rented single-storey bungalow in Petaling Jaya. My housemates were Chinese, Indian and Malay. We were a microcosm of Malaysia's racial mix. As the riots raged and smoke billowed from burning houses some distance away, each of us wondered to himself: if we were attacked by a mob, Chinese or Malay, would we protect one another, and probably die in the process, or stand by as the mob attacked one or more of us? We were good friends, having studied abroad together under Colombo Plan scholarships and working at Telecoms Malaysia to serve our scholarship bonds.

Fortunately, our loyalties to one another were never tested.

But the ordeal of living in fear under a curfew with violence and killing around us left a psychological scar. Little could I have guessed then that those traumatic two weeks would prove to be a turning point in my life.

Shortly after the incident, I asked for a transfer to Johor Bahru to be further away from the epicentre of racial unrest. I had time to mull over my future in the racially torn society that Malaysia had become and wondered if I could still pursue a meaningful career in the country of my birth.

I chanced upon an advertisement in *The Straits Times*. The Economic Development Board (EDB) of Singapore was recruiting Project Officers for investment evaluation. I applied for a position, intending it to be an interim move to a safer place until the political situation settled down in Malaysia. I was 25 years old and had a whole life ahead of me. I was accepted into the EDB and swept headlong into a dynamic Singapore society and rigorous work culture. There never was time to look back, although I have never forgotten my roots in Malaysia.

I keep in touch with economic and social developments there and maintain contacts with old classmates. Many of us have emigrated overseas, to Australia, Singapore and the US. Today we have a chat group for "EC62", whose members graduated from Higher School Certificate class (equivalent of Junior College) in 1962 from English College, Johor Bahru. During our college years, we hardly noticed our racial differences and enjoyed sincere good fellowship, something that has sadly diminished in Malaysia over the last five decades. We love Malaysia and fervently hope to see it develop some day into a modern state with racial and social harmony.

Career Resilience

I grew up in a shophouse in Muar, Johor with six siblings. My parents taught in local Chinese schools. With such a large family, they did not have much time for each of us individually. We pursued our intellectual curiosities by reading. Among my prized possessions was *Pears Cyclopaedia*, a compendium of information from Greek mythology to the marine life of the Antarctica. My first history book was from a popular bookshop Tuck's Store. I had dipped into my meagre savings accumulated from cutting back on lunch spending and purchased Hendrik van Loon's *The Story of Mankind* in 1956 for a princely sum of $1.20. I still have the book, its pages yellow and desiccated but remaining a delight to read.

There were many books on European and British history, but precious little was available on local Malayan history. So, we grew up understanding little of our Asian heritage, how Chinese and Indian immigrants had contributed to the development of Malaya, how the British colonial regime had shaped our lives for better and for worse.

My parents emigrated to Malaya in their early 1920s from the Quanzhou area of Fujian province in China. As educators with Confucian upbringings, they inculcated in us a love of learning. Looking back at my life, this was the greatest gift that I received from them. It inspired me to study hard and win a coveted scholarship abroad. It launched me on a long and winding path in which the only constant was continually learning new skills and acquiring knowledge.

Lifelong learning enabled me to change career several times, reinventing myself each time. A passion for learning meant that

I could change careers by eagerly studying a new discipline. Love of learning bestowed on me the gift of career resilience.

After my stint in Malaysian Telecoms and the EDB Singapore, I spent two years at General Electric (USA) as a quality control engineer, then production manager. I developed an interest in economics and left to pursue graduate studies in the United States. Upon graduation, I taught for a while at the Kellogg School of Management in Chicago before returning to Singapore to take up a faculty position at the then University of Singapore. From there I started a 20-year career in business, culminating as President and Chief Executive Officer of the diversified listed company Haw Par Corporation Limited.

Halfway through my corporate career, anticipating a sojourn into politics, I took a year off to attend the Master of Public Administration programme at Harvard. At age 42, I was inducted into the People's Action Party (PAP) and later served a term as a PAP Member of Parliament for Bedok Group Representation Constituency (GRC). I gained unexpected notoriety by chairing the Parliamentary Select Committee for Land Transport which proposed the vehicle quota system, later implemented as the Certificate of Entitlement (COE) scheme.

After retiring from Haw Par, I was appointed Dean of the College of Business at Nanyang Technological University (NTU) where I served full-time until 2012, when I retired to an adjunct professor position.

While at Haw Par and NTU, I developed an avid interest in Chinese culture and Chinese medicine, studied part-time and earned graduate degrees in Chinese literature as well as Chinese medicine. My newfound knowledge and skills helped launch me into my fourth career, practising and writing about Chinese medicine.

During those years when I was chief executive at Haw Par Corporation, I travelled extensively to China, particularly Shanghai, Suzhou and Beijing, and greatly improved my command of spoken Mandarin. Although I studied part-time for the bachelor's and master's degrees in Chinese language and literature from Beijing Normal University, it was the use of spoken Mandarin with both personal and business friends in China that gave me a feel for the idiomatic use of the language. I learned as much Mandarin from shooting the breeze (*liaotian*) with these friends as I did from formal studies.

I strongly recommend to everyone who wants to gain command of Mandarin to use it often in daily conversation and not just stick to rote learning from textbooks, formal courses and tutors. The best tuition in Mandarin is to be found in watching high-quality television historical dramas from China, and in small talk and belting out Mandarin lyrics in karaoke lounges over glasses of cold beer.

After retiring from full-time work at NTU, I fulfilled a lifelong wish to study philosophy. I did a one-year master's degree in the history and philosophy of science in Cambridge before starting a doctoral thesis at the London School of Economics and Political Science, completing it at the age of 68. I was thrilled to study in the department founded by the renowned Sir Karl Popper, philosopher of science and of political thought. His *magnum opus* on the philosophy of science, *The Logic of Scientific Discovery*, and his celebrated assault on totalitarianism in *The Open Society and its Enemies* remain among the most read books on philosophy.

Studying Western philosophy deepened my understanding of Chinese medicine, which is both a science of healing as well as the art and philosophy of life cultivation. My doctoral dissertation was expanded into a book, *Principles of Chinese Medicine: A Modern Interpretation* (Imperial College Press, 2016), in which I provide an interpretation of Chinese medical theory from the viewpoint of modern biomedical science. Three other books followed on the scientific and cultural aspects of Chinese medicine for the general reader.

Philosophy brought together all my other educational disciplines – engineering, economics, literature and Chinese medicine. I believe that in the higher reaches of knowledge all disciplines find common ground in logic, rationality and order in the universes that exist outside and within us, as well as a spiritual dimension that transcends materialism.

Identity Resilience

Going through the turbulent period of racial tensions in Malaysia in 1969 heightened my consciousness of being Chinese. It was the beginning of a journey of self-discovery which fortified personal resilience by allowing me to know and be comfortable with my own identity and my place in society.

Growing up in colonial Malaya and receiving an English education while brought up by Chinese-educated parents can easily give a person cultural schizophrenia. I loved English literature, idolised Western movie stars and pop singers, and was seduced by liberal democratic ideals – to the extent that at the age of 16 I won a state oratorical contest recounting the life and times of Abraham Lincoln. I even proudly recited part of his

Gettysburg address: *Government of the people, for the people, and by the people, shall not perish from the earth.*

Yet at home my father, a Chinese school headmaster, was a role model for me. He ardently supported the Chinese revolution of 1949 that propelled Mao and the authoritarian Communist Party to power. I cheered with him when the mighty Americans were humiliated into calling for a truce after they failed to vanquish the poor and technologically backward Chinese in the Korean War.

I resolved this internal conflict of ideologies later in life when I realised that there is no truth in the American mythology that a single political system (liberal democracy) should prevail across different cultures in the world. In my recent book *The Rule of Culture: Corporate and State Governance in China and East Asia* (Routledge, 2020), I suggest that benign authoritarian governance has worked well in China up to now because that country is steeped in 2,500 years of Confucian culture. But I also acknowledge that today only liberal democracy is acceptable to Western cultures like those of France and America, even if unfettered freedom comes at the price of disorderly and dysfunctional societies.

The Malaysian racial riots of 1969 were a rude cultural awakening. I realised that despite my Western education my core values were Asian, the Malayan Chinese version of it. Being culturally Chinese did not mean that I could not be a loyal citizen of multiracial Malaysia, or that I could not appreciate and live alongside other cultures. What I found hard to accept was not being a first-class citizen in the country in which I was born and brought up. A similar sentiment surfaced eight years later when, after two years' teaching in Chicago, US immigration laws required me to either leave the country or take up permanent residence to continue my academic career. My dean persuaded me to stay and build a career in the US. But I could not bring myself to live permanently in a country where I was culturally an alien. There was no overt racial discrimination in the university at which I taught, as the teaching faculty was truly international. Also, in the 1970s people in Chicago were generally friendly to Asians.

But underneath the genteel politeness of local Americans, I sometimes sensed that either I was being patronised or there lurked a hint of xenophobia. Except among close colleagues within the university faculty, I would often feel that l was a guest in the country, treated nicely or poorly at the pleasure of my hosts.

Since the meteoric rise of China in the 21st century and the noisily disruptive Trump phenomenon of 2016, people of Chinese origin in the US are increasingly resented and sometimes treated with brashness, even violence. US political leaders want desperately to preserve American hegemony in the face of their own economic decline and a rising China. Their feeling of insecurity is understandable but, instead of pulling up their socks, they stoop low to demonise Chinese governance in the name of protecting Western democratic values. All they are really trying to protect are the luxury of bullying weak nations with impunity and the economic privilege of world hegemony, including printing the US dollar to finance the country's spending beyond its means.

I realise now that I made the right decision some 40 years

ago not to settle down in the US, or it would have profoundly pained me now to witness the angst and suspicion with which mainstream America views people of Chinese origin. I am pleased and grateful that I live in Singapore, where I do not have to apologise for being Chinese.

The PAP government in Singapore is currently going through soul searching to understand why it lost ground in the last general election (10 July 2020) despite holding all the cards for electoral advantage. These included a near $100 billion spend from government coffers to rescue the economy and save jobs, and the prohibition of mass rallies in which alternative parties traditionally have been able to attract and mobilise large crowds. I am hopeful that with wisdom and empathy, the PAP will emerge chastened and reinvigorated to continue the wise policies of multiracialism, meritocracy and strong leadership that have enabled Singapore to progress from third to first world in one generation.

In Singapore, an Indian, Malay or Chinese does not suffer racial discrimination by the government. They can be proud of their ethnicity without compromising loyalty to the country. They can be an Indian Singaporean, a Malay Singaporean or a Chinese Singaporean, but first a Singaporean. This state of racial harmony has been the most significant achievement of the post-Independence government.

In its wisdom, the Singapore Government has encouraged each racial group to be proud of and appreciate its own ethnic culture, as that provides a secure anchor for an essential part of their complex identity. At the same time, we celebrate and thrive in a common Singapore culture which includes *nasi lemak*, *char kuay teow*, *roti prata*, *kiasuism* and an obsessive penchant for cleanliness, orderliness and predictability.

We have learned over the last 60 years to increasingly tolerate and appreciate each ethnic group's peculiarities, charm and unique strengths. Few other nations in the world have been able to achieve this. I hope we continue to be a beacon to the world of interracial harmony, where each citizen is comfortable with their ethnicity yet can identify themselves as Singaporeans, loyal to the country. Being comfortable in our own skins is an important part of one's individual resilience.

In time, there surely will be a gradual fusion of ethnic cultures, and a distinct Singapore cultural identity will emerge. Even then, ethnic identities will still be there, but coexist with the Singapore identity in a healthy and harmonious, even colourful and exciting way.

ABOUT HONG HAI

Hong Hai is Emeritus Professor and former Dean of the College of Business at the Nanyang Technological University, Member of the Singapore Parliament, and Chief Executive of Haw Par Corporation. Now a part-time practising physician in traditional Chinese medicine, he is a polymath who embodies the virtues of learning and humility. The quintessential professor, his unwavering commitment to education is a testament to his purpose-driven life.

Education in the Era of Disruptive Technology[1]

Cham Tao Soon

Over time, the way we do business and lifestyle has changed. The changes will become more rapid with the frequent use of computers aided by artificial intelligence (AI). This age of disruptive technology is sometimes called Industry 4.0.

The first Industrial Revolution was attributed to the development of the steam engine which transformed agrarian societies to industrial economies. The initial benefactors were the textile industries that became mechanised. Then came the improvements in transportation as applied to vehicles.

The Second Industrial Revolution was attributed to the development of electricity used for electric motor technology, convenient household use and telecommunication. Automation in factories was further enhanced.

---

[1] The essay is a slight modification of his lecture at the Inaugural Annual Lecture of the National University of Science and Technology, Oman in 2019. The lecture was attended by the Deputy Prime Minister and his Cabinet Ministers.

Industry 3.0 introduced computerisation for information and communication technology (ICT). The Internet was able to connect everyone all over the world for business or for social purposes.

Now, Industry 4.0 represents new ways in which technology becomes embedded within societies, driven by advances in computers, AI and automation. Both work and lifestyles will undergo significant changes.

Some experts predict that it will make half the population jobless very quickly because robots or digital transformations will take over all the tasks. I have a different view. The steam engine, electricity and Internet did not cause mass unemployment overnight. The changes forced people to adjust quickly. So too will be the case for the present generation.

We have to accept there will be great changes to the way we work and our lifestyles. That is inevitable. To meet the challenges, our students have to be equipped with skills through education and training.

We can no longer rely on traditional education methods of just broadening the minds. Machines are becoming more intelligent than humans, and with their ability to store large amounts of information, the machines are more knowledgeable than all of us. We need a different strategy of preparing our students so that they are better than the machines in other ways.

I believe we need an immediate as well as a long-term strategy in education to succeed in this era of disruptive technology.

Immediate Strategy

For immediate implementation, we need to enhance the skills of our students to be able to make use of the power of computers and machines rather than to compete with them. To do that, the core knowledge needed would be in information technology (IT) and robotic engineering.

AI is related to the ability of machines for general learning and high-level reasoning, which are cognitive functions associated only with humans. The key to the success of AI is good computer programming on powerful computing machines. To develop our students towards those skills, we may need to review our high school curriculum. It may be necessary to include in all streams of studies a good grounding in mathematics and also sciences. This will not be a unique system as it has been practised in the French high school system since the days of Napoleon. The additional knowledge in mathematics and science will help young students understand the abilities of computers.

At a higher level, at polytechnics and universities, all streams of studies need to include modules on IT and data analytics. IT is the basis of the intelligent world. It comprises disciplines such as internet communication, Internet of Things (sensors), virtual reality and digital network for data communication.

It is difficult to avoid 'big data'. With the power of the Internet of Things, fast computers and enormous data storage capacity, data accumulates at a tremendous pace. From data, information is constructed. Collections of related data give insights into useful knowledge. If the knowledge is targeted, solutions to problems can be devised. So, data analytics has been applied in many areas such as business decisions and logistics, and it's a powerful scientific tool.

These tools are needed not just for technical people. Professionals such as doctors and lawyers will also need to rely on such expertise for their daily work in the future. Examples are in disease identification using AI, medical robotics, legal case searches using AI, language translation of legal documents, and so on.

Other than equipping our students with technical skills, higher education needs to be more targeted towards professional practices and careers. Our universities and polytechnics should provide their students with more channels for internships which would cultivate students to be more market-oriented. Businesses should be more proactive in welcoming students to their companies. Our present national strategy of re-skill and up-skill, and SkillsFuture are in line with the need to adapt to the challenges of disruptive technology. We have to note that skill in this context does not refer to "manual" skill only, but should include "knowledge" skill.

I like to re-emphasise the importance of acquiring skills for the future education of students and workers. We need to have the skill to make use of the power of computers since we cannot compete with its intelligence. That is, we need problem-solving skills as the best approach to get the outcomes.

Looking at Singapore's education system, I think polytechnic education is best suited for problem solving. I venture to predict the best path for our students in the future is to go through a polytechnic training first before going to the university. The German education system has a similar philosophy.

Long-term Strategy

For the long-term learning strategy, there are three aspects of formal education we need to emphasise. The first is the cultivation of creativity. Many people think that the human ability to come up with a new idea is better than machines. Ultimately, computers lack imagination or creativity to dream up a vision for the future. It lacks the emotional competence that a human has.

Thus, creativity will be the skill of the future. The key to staying ahead and participating in the creation of the future is our own creativity. We must embrace and develop our creativity, and then use technology creatively to solve problems of the world.

Our education system must nurture creativity of students. This cannot be achieved by just learning facts to come up with new insights. I believe the best way to promote creativity is through open-ended projects. It is even better if projects are performed by a team. The interactions of members often generate new ideas and new approaches to problem solving.

The second requirement of higher education in this new age is to be able to mould students to be good members of society. Students have to learn the art of giving and taking. This behaviour is superior to machines, which have no moral agency and can act only through a prescribed programme.

The education path is to develop emotional quotient (EQ) and not just intelligence quotient (IQ). EQ is the capability of individuals to recognise their own emotions and those of others and use such information to guide their thinking and behaviour.

Education modules should include studies on ethics, self-awareness, self-control, social skills and empathy. I am aware such skills are difficult to impart. This is often achieved through inspirational lectures or case studies and practical acts such as visiting old folks' homes and homes for the disadvantaged. Parents can also help at home by being role models.

The third requirement of a future education system is to include a strong emphasis on lifelong learning. This is becoming more urgent as time passes. New technologies and new concepts are introduced constantly. Knowledge will become obsolete very quickly and therefore, continuous learning is needed to make oneself relevant. To enable learners to keep up, using e-learning is a good platform.

All public and private bodies need to have e-learning facilities as well as support services to make such learning methods easy to use.

Conclusion

To sum up, education in the era of disruptive technology needs to incorporate learnings on skills to take advantage of the intelligence of machines as well as teachings in creativity, development in EQ and an effective system of continuous education. These are means to make humans better than machines. Until we have an effective strategy on education, we would be left behind by Industry 4.0.

A concluding note is that even in a world full of powerful hardware, software and networks, people remain valuable because of their judgement and reasoning beyond calculations and data. Therefore, it is important that they have the best education in knowledge and skill.

ABOUT CHAM TAO SOON

The author is essentially an engineer by training and had his BE at the University of Malaya as a Singapore State Scholar. He went on to complete his academic training at the University of Cambridge with a PhD. His contribution to Singapore was, however, in the start-up of universities. Of the six public universities in Singapore he was involved in the start-up and development of three of them: Nanyang Technological University, Singapore Management University and Singapore University of Social Sciences. In fact, he was the inaugural President of NTU for 21 years from 1981 to 2002. His career included directorships in Keppel Corp, Wearne Brothers, Natsteel, Robinsons, ST Engineering, Singapore Press Holdings, SMRT, Land Transport Authority and UOB. He was at one time President of the Institution of Engineers Singapore and President, Academy of Engineering Singapore.

Taking the Long View[1]

Tan Yong Soon

I feel very honoured to return to my alma mater as Guest of Honour at its 184th Founder's Day. The last Raffles Institution (RI) Founder's Day I attended was in 1972, 35 years ago, under very different circumstances.

In 1972, Singapore was poor. The Singapore economy was further threatened by the withdrawal of British Forces from Singapore. But Singapore not only converted the empty naval bases into shipyards which grew into successful conglomerates, it also stepped up its industrialisation programme.

In the ensuing decades of nation building, Singapore had to continually rise to new challenges of various forms. When the long-term availability of imported water was uncertain, we reclaimed used water and developed NEWater which allows us to be self-sufficient in our water supply should the need arise.

---

[1] Tan Yong Soon delivered this speech on 26 May 2007 as the Guest of Honour at Raffles Institution's 184th Founder's Day. He was Permanent Secretary in the Ministry of the Environment and Water Resources.

We are now a world leader in cutting-edge water technologies. Many countries have come to Singapore, wanting to collaborate with and learn from us.

As Singapore grew quickly and talent was in short supply, we ramped up skills development of our citizens and also welcomed foreigners and the return of overseas Singaporeans who had left to work or live abroad.

Singapore has succeeded and prospered because of the vision and courage of its leaders, as well as the commitment and hard work of its people. Singapore has often been decisive and courageous in taking innovative action. In our plans and policies, we have always taken the long view to ensure that we take care of ourselves not only for the present, but also for the future generations that follow.

Let me use the environment as an example. In 1972, the Singapore Government established the Ministry of the Environment. This was immediately after the United Nations Conference on the Human Environment in Stockholm in June 1972. The Stockholm Conference was itself an environmental watershed as it was the first international forum that was aimed at addressing global environmental challenges. And Singapore was one of the first countries to form a ministry dedicated to creating and sustaining a good environment for its people.

Singapore demonstrated our commitment because we have always believed that a good environment not only contributes to a higher quality of life, but also promotes economic development that would further enhance standards of living. Recognising the importance of Singapore's environment to our long-term development, we took key steps to preserve and enhance it right from the start, so that the economy and the environment could progress in tandem.

As a result of these efforts, among others, Singapore has been consistently rated best for the overall quality of our environment among Asian countries for the past six years in the international survey by the Political and Economic Risk Consultancy (PERC). The quality of our environment has helped us to raise the standard of living for Singaporeans and continually attract talent, investments and tourists to our shores.

In a similar manner, RI has braved the challenges and emerged stronger than before. In the late 60s and early 70s, with the rapid expansion of our educational system, RI had to endure many of its best teachers being taken away to head the many new schools created. There was also a challenge of new junior colleges (JCs), starting with National Junior College (NJC) in 1969. And a number of RI's top students had left RI to attend NJC. Thirty-five years later, RI has continued to retain its pre-eminent position and now has less to worry about its students moving on to other JCs.

In 1972, many of my friends grew up very poor, but we all benefited as Singapore progressed and prospered, growing from a per capita GDP of US$1,354 in 1972 to US$29,474 in 2006 – a remarkable 22 times.

Indeed, we have lived the Singapore Dream. Some have fared better than others. Those who succeeded inevitably have the following pre-requisites:

a. capacity to work hard
b. willingness to learn from everyone
c. good people skills and work through people

d. resilience to stress and determination in adversity

e. triumph over life's imperfections and readiness to put failure behind them

f. passion and persistence in the pursuit of goals

g. courage to venture out of comfort zone to take risks and seize opportunities; and probably most import of all;

h. a rich network of friends developed from young.

Singapore and many of my fellow Rafflesian friends have had to brave many challenges to our survival and success, and through it all we have succeeded and grown stronger. Crises have made us stronger.

Looking ahead, Singapore will be continually faced with even greater challenges. Increasing globalisation and the integration of economies across countries offer great opportunity for people to tap into more and larger markets around the world. Singapore has benefited from globalisation and reached First World status. We now have to compete with First World economies. We have to be able to continue competing on this higher plane, or risk being marginalised. This means we must become better and more innovative.

Times have changed and yet many challenges remain. Thirty-five years ago, RI had to shoulder a great responsibility as the pre-eminent school in Singapore – it had to educate and groom leaders for a country that was taking its first steps towards independence. Today, it is still developing leaders, albeit for a new set of challenges.

Youth and young adults can take greater interest in the critical issues of the day. I know that this is already starting to take place, with interest translated not just into academic projects, but into everyday actions and lifestyle changes. In the area of environment, these include recycling, conserving electricity and water, and keeping public places clean.

In this respect, I am heartened to note that Rafflesians are also leading the way. I read in the May 2007 issue of *RInspire* that environmental champion Samuel Lim attended the ASEAN Youth Forum on the Environment early this year, clinched the silver award in the TechChallenge Competition, and resolved to continue working for the betterment of the environment.

Last year, four Secondary 4 students won the 2006 Green Wave Award (secondary school category) for their project on turning fruit peels into paper, which is an example of creative problem solving as well as demonstrating a strong sense of environmental conservation and awareness of recycling. And RI is also one of the pioneer schools to have set up a recycling corner in Singapore.

As we go forward, the best of Singaporeans must be equal to the best in the world if Singapore, a small island state with no natural resources other than its people, is to succeed. I would urge you to have the confidence to be as good as, if not better than, any in the world. The future is challenging but it is also more exciting. The world is your oyster and the sky is literally the limit. But when you have succeeded, always remember the source of your drinking water and contribute to the community.

And I would urge you to continue to be environmentally responsible in whichever leadership role you assume in the future, be it in public service, business or as part of your community. In so doing, we can all do our part to bring about a better age.

Nurturing Tomorrow's Leaders

Tan Eng Chye

The National University of Singapore (NUS) has been at the forefront of educational innovation, continuously evolving its curriculum to meet the demands of the 21st century. With a commitment to nurturing future-ready leaders who are lifelong learners, NUS has established an educational framework that is broad-based, flexible and interdisciplinary, with an emphasis on real-world problem-solving.

What an NUS Education Offers

The General Education component lies at the foundation of the NUS undergraduate curriculum, with the aim of fostering breadth of learning by preparing students to think deeply, ask critical questions and discuss issues relating to the diverse and dynamic cultural landscape. First introduced in 2001, it has been periodically reformed over the years to ensure its relevance to the changing needs of the work environment.

As Singapore's flagship university that was founded by the community, for the community, a key aspect of NUS' culture and practice is giving back to the community. The **Singapore Studies** and the **Communities and Engagement** pillars help guide students to address the needs of communities by participating in activities to uplift those around them. Teach Singapore (Teach SG), a University-wide initiative where NUS students provide academic coaching and mentoring to children and youth from lower-income families, is now a credit-bearing practicum under the Communities and Engagement pillar.

To nurture culturally aware citizens who are effective communicators, there are the **Critique and Expression**, and the **Cultures and Connections** pillars. These also lay the groundwork which students can flesh out through future project work, presentations, global experiences, and other learning activities. Most recently, **Data Literacy** and **Digital Literacy** have been included as part of general education. This is to align with Industry 4.0, which is highly data-driven and technology-centric.

Beyond general education, a common curriculum is in place for all undergraduate students, mostly within the same faculty, school or college. It allows students to gain exposure across traditional disciplines as well as emerging fields, and the application to current problems. While this approach pivots from providing students with comprehensive knowledge in their major – the major requirement had to be condensed to 15 courses (for most majors) – the broad academic exposure hones intellectual versatility and builds the capacity to engage in lifelong learning.

To illustrate, the Common Curriculum for Healthcare Professional Education was developed for undergraduates in the

Table 1. Overview of NUS' common curriculum and how the General Education Pillars fit in

NUS Common Curriculum (between 10 and 15 courses)	
General Education Pillars (6 courses)	Singapore Studies, Cultures & Connections, Communities & Engagement, Critique & Expression, Data Literacy, Digital Literacy
College/Faculty/ School Pillars (between 4 and 9 courses)	Specific to the individual college, faculty or school

health science disciplines, namely Medicine, Dentistry, Nursing and Pharmacy. This was done to sufficiently prepare students for future healthcare challenges, such as an ageing population and the increasing use of data and digital technologies in healthcare. In this regard, the existing medical curriculum had to be reduced, mainly by completely restructuring the first two years of the curriculum.

Through flexible pathways, students have greater agency to pursue a wide range of majors, second majors, minors, specialisations, and cross-disciplinary programmes to deepen their expertise or learn multiple competencies. For example, an unrestricted elective component created by the NUS Faculty of Law allows students to broaden through a second major or minor, while Engineering students can now pick up knowledge and skills on design thinking and sustainability through their interdisciplinary common curriculum. These curriculum changes were made in consultation with relevant professional bodies. Whether they choose depth or breadth, students have the choice and are highly encouraged to return to the University as alumni to broaden or deepen their knowledge through continuing education offerings.

Finally, there has been a concerted move to interdisciplinary learning to complement disciplinary training in response to the rapidly and ever-changing workplace that is volatile, uncertain, complex and ambiguous (VUCA) in nature. Empowering students to combine frameworks and concepts across multiple disciplines will allow them to examine themes from different perspectives or devise solutions that transcend the boundaries of disciplines. Learning is amplified when students harness and integrate knowledge and approaches. It will also foster creativity, encourage the exploration of new ideas and enhance complex problem-solving.

A significant milestone to scale interdisciplinary teaching and learning at NUS was the establishment of the College of Humanities and Sciences (CHS) in 2020, which spans both the Faculty of Arts and Social Sciences and the Faculty of Science. It offers students 13 courses as part of its common curriculum, or one-third of the total curriculum, consisting of Common Core Courses, Integrated Courses, and Interdisciplinary Courses. These are designed to help students build strong foundational skills such as reading, writing, critical thinking and numeracy, as well as develop the traits of adaptability, resilience and empathy. Students are also trained to think, synthesise and integrate knowledge and insights across disciplines towards solving complex problems.

Table 2. An overview of the curriculum for the College of Humanities and Sciences (CHS)

CHS Curriculum		
Common Curriculum	**Major Requirements**	**Unrestricted Electives**
13 courses	15 courses	12 courses

Table 3. Details of CHS' common curriculum, which comprises 13 courses, or one-third of the total curriculum. There are three components – Common Core Courses, Integrated Courses and Interdisciplinary Courses.

CHS Common Curriculum		
Common Core / General Education (6 courses)	**Integrated Pillars (5 courses)**	**Interdisciplinary Pillars (2 courses)**
Artificial Intelligence	Asian Studies	Interdisciplinary Course I
Communities & Engagement	Humanities	Interdisciplinary Course II
Design Thinking	Scientific Inquiry I	
Writing	Scientific Inquiry II	
Data Literacy	Social Sciences	
Digital Literacy		

Figures 1 to 3 (from left to right): Flexibility allows CHS students to chart their own pathway

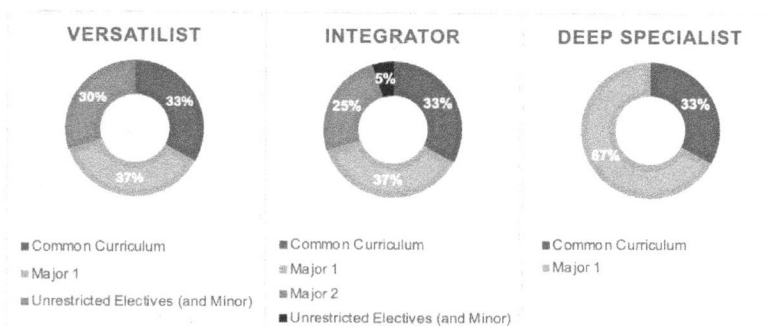

VERSATILIST	INTEGRATOR	DEEP SPECIALIST
30% 33% 37%	5% 25% 33% 37%	33% 67%
■ Common Curriculum	■ Common Curriculum	■ Common Curriculum
■ Major 1	■ Major 1	■ Major 1
■ Unrestricted Electives (and Minor)	■ Major 2	
	■ Unrestricted Electives (and Minor)	

Since then, two other interdisciplinary colleges have been formed – the College of Design and Engineering, which fused the Faculty of Engineering and the School of Design and Environment, and NUS College, Singapore's first Honours College.

Building Capacity for More Ts

Cognisant that the aim is to prepare students for their careers, there is an emphasis on ensuring that students have a strong disciplinary foundation. They will then be able to build and rebuild their disciplinary knowledge and skills even after their graduation and as the field and industry develop, through continuing education and training.

This aligns with the move from a T-shaped model of learning, which stressed a singular domain specialisation, to a "π" approach, which involves straddling two majors or a major and minor combination or other flexible forms of domain knowledge acquisition. The broad-based, flexible and self-directed pathways in the revised undergraduate curriculum empower students in building more Ts and prepare our graduates for multiple reskilling and upskilling as they progress through their careers. This is crucial given that careers now last 40 to 50 years and much of the discipline-related knowledge and skills will become obsolete at a faster pace. Acquiring more Ts also hedges our graduates for disruptions, as they would be able to pivot more easily.

Global Experiential Learning Opportunities

NUS provides undergraduate students with a range of international opportunities to expand their horizon such as student exchanges, overseas community engagement programmes and global internships. NUS Overseas Colleges, our flagship entrepreneurship programme, nurtures enterprising, resourceful and independent self-starters by immersing them in start-up hubs around the world.

Launched in 2023 is the Southeast Asia Friendship Initiative (SFI), which adds to the array of global programmes. With a focus on the United Nations Sustainable Development Goals (UNSDGs), SFI exposes students to real issues and challenges faced by Southeast Asian communities, while fostering a deeper appreciation of the diverse cultures, histories and complexities in the region. Students from various NUS halls, residential colleges and houses embarked on the inaugural experiential study trips from May to July 2023.

Developing a Holistic University Experience

Since 2021, NUS has embarked on a narrative to prioritise student life as an integral part of education which we believe has an intrinsic value in enhancing our students' university experience.

Student life encompasses out-of-classroom learning opportunities beyond the formal curriculum that take place through residential programmes, co-curricular activities, sports and the arts, community engagement, and the promotion of student physical and mental well-being. These platforms serve as the wellspring for developing life skills that complete the academic training to better equip our graduates for a more disruptive and uncertain future.

To integrate the arts into undergraduate learning, NUS recently launched the Arts For All (AFA) framework that will give students the option to earn academic credits for year-long courses that can fulfil elective requirements of their undergraduate education or be stacked towards a Minor or Second Major in Performing Arts. This is an upgrade from credit-bearing performing arts courses that were introduced in August 2023.

To bolster a more holistic university experience, NUSOne, a roadmap to access and discover the diverse range of student life activities, will be built into the undergraduate programme from the Academic Year 2024/2025.

The "Transition to Higher Education" (T.H.E) programme for first-year students will familiarise them with the essentials of university education to smoothen their transition and help them navigate the non-academic informal learning space early in their university journey. The programme seeks to build character and hone life skills such as integrity, leadership, adaptability and resilience through active engagement in co-curricular activities, be it arts and culture, sports, community service or advocacy for social causes.

Conclusion

Emerging technologies, especially artificial intelligence, will transform industries and bring about disruptions to jobs. In the face of relentless change, NUS needs to equip our graduates with the relevant skills, aptitudes and attitudes so that they can thrive and sustain in their careers. We are steadfast in our purpose to cultivate agile, innovative and resilient lifelong learners who have a deep conviction to make positive impact, for the students of today will be the leaders of tomorrow.

ABOUT TAN ENG CHYE

Tan Eng Chye is Professor and currently President of the National University of Singapore (NUS). Appointed on 1 January 2018, he is the University's 5th president, and the 23rd leader to head Singapore's oldest higher education institution. An NUS alumnus and mathematician by training, Professor Tan is a passionate and award-winning educator who has contributed significantly to the design of NUS' current academic system and seeded many of its educational initiatives. In recognition of his outstanding contributions in the areas of academia, education and leadership, Professor Tan has been awarded the Public Administration Medal (Gold) at Singapore's National Day Awards (2014), the Wilbur Lucius Cross Medal by Yale University (2018), an Honorary Doctor of Science from the University of Southampton (2018) and an Honorary Doctor of Management from Universiti Malaya (2023), amongst others.

PART 4

WHAT DO YOU SEEK?

D o you seek success or happiness or both? It would depend on how we understand what success and happiness are.

Aristotle is quoted as having said, "All men seek one goal: success or happiness." He added, however, "The only way to achieve true success is to express yourself completely in service to society."

Success is not measured in wealth or power, but in service to society, in finding the best in others, in leaving the world a bit better and making a difference. Every one of us can achieve success and satisfaction in our different ways.

Part 4 explores success, happiness and friendship. Friendship is one of the most important virtues in achieving the goal of happiness. In fact, Aristotle valued friendship very highly, and described a "virtuous" friendship as the most enjoyable, combining both pleasure and virtue. However, a broken friendship can be very painful as depicted in the movie *The Banshees of Inisherin*, when Colm feels that his time chatting with Padraic has been a meaningless distraction from creating art that will outlast him.

This book ends with an abridged version of an interview on leadership with Mr J.Y. Pillay, conducted by Viswa Sadasivan in 2015. The excerpt is reproduced here with J.Y. Pillay's permission. J.Y. Pillay is one of the pioneers who helped build the Singapore economy and public service after its independence in 1965, having served as a Permanent Secretary in a few ministries, the first Chairman of Singapore Airlines between 1972 and 1996, and Chairman of the Council of Presidential Advisers between 2005 and 2019. I have used the full transcript to discuss leadership with my students. J.Y. Pillay has himself come to my class in the initial years to share his insights and experience with my students.

CHAPTER 15

Success

O ne day in class, a Master of Public Administration (MPA) student asked me what achievement I was most proud of. He asked if it was being promoted to Permanent Secretary, the highest civil service position. I do not deny the satisfaction of being appointed as Permanent Secretary, reaching the apex of the civil service career. It was also humbling, realising the great responsibility that came with the job. But success is not achieved via a promotion, a higher job title or greater authority. Success is measured by the impact that we leave behind as a leader (beyond the public policies), how well we serve the public and how we prepare for future challenges.

Everyone Has a Part to Play

I was very proud of the impact I was able to leave behind when I was the Perm Sec of the Ministry of the Environment and Water Resources (MEWR), but I would also be proud had I been a director or in some other position in the ministry and not its Perm Sec. It was immensely gratifying to be able to work with the staff from the ministry and the Public Utilities Board (PUB), the national water agency, in developing water technology, increasing water capacity, growing a vibrant and sustainable water and environment industry, and ensuring the long-term water self-sufficiency for Singapore. Everyone played a part in the achievement. Success has indeed many fathers.

Similarly, it was gratifying working with the National Climate Change Secretariat staff and various government agencies in developing Singapore's strategy and strengthening the national climate change structure and capabilities to meet the challenges in climate change. Or working with Urban Redevelopment Authority (URA) staff to make Singapore a great city in which to live, work and play. Or even as an infantry company commander leading 100-odd soldiers, mostly full-time National Servicemen (NSFs), looking after their welfare and making sure they were well trained, knowing that we were playing a part in the security of Singapore.

Many major projects and policies require inter-agency coordination and are long term in nature. While a project may have been completed successfully or a policy announced at a point in time, many people are involved in the gestation period and many continue to be involved in its implementation. We stand on the shoulders of our predecessors, some of whom are giants, and at the same time we are laying the groundwork for those who come after us. Marina Barrage was completed, the first desalinated water plant became operational and NEWater plants added during my time in MEWR, but the foundations were laid decades and years earlier.

There is great satisfaction when we make the right policy. We studied the UK privatisation of water and sewage disposal system. We also learned from the Water Services Regulation Authority, or Ofwat, responsible for setting the price regime that water companies are required to follow and for monitoring performance of the new water companies. We decided against privatisation. The PUB would retain control on quality, quantity and pricing. Private sector companies were invited to build and operate water plants through a DBOO (design, build, own, operate) model. Public-private partnership arrangements through DBOO reap efficiency gains, are also valuable and highly strategic learning opportunities for private companies to interact with the government agency over an extended period of time, tapping each other's amassed expertise and experience. But we ensured contractual measures were structured to ensure that the quantity and quality of water supply met required standards. The PUB could step in in the event the concession company failed or was in default.

Likewise with many issues involving the environment, climate change, urban planning, finance and defence work which I had been involved in, everyone has a part to play, whatever his level.

Success can be measured in different ways: our career highlights, personal milestones, individual growth. Success can also be measured by how much better we are when compared with others or how we compare with our past self. How we have improved ourselves and how we have helped others. How well we have lived.

<u>What is success</u>? Bessie Stanley wrote the poem below in 1904 for a magazine contest. The competition was to answer the question "What is success?" in 100 words or less. Mrs Stanley won the first prize of $250.

—◦◉◉◦—

Success
by
Bessie Anderson Stanley

He has achieved success
who has lived well,
laughed often, and loved much;

who has enjoyed the trust of
pure women,

the respect of intelligent men and
the love of little children;

who has filled his niche and accomplished his task;

who has left the world better than he found it
whether by an improved poppy,
a perfect poem or a rescued soul;

who has never lacked appreciation of Earth's beauty
or failed to express it;

who has always looked for the best in others and
given them the best he had;

whose life was an inspiration;
whose memory a benediction.

———•◦◉◦•———

The original poem, slightly modified in a version we commonly see today, is often misattributed to Ralph Waldo Emerson.

The poem is powerful. At a tender age of 25, Bessie understood that success is not measured in wealth or power, but in joy and making a difference. "To appreciate beauty; to find the best in others; to leave the world a bit better, whether by a healthy child, a garden patch or a redeemed social condition; to know even one life has breathed easier because you have lived. This is to have succeeded!" Each of these acts is a success. Every one of us, whether a private or a general, a junior clerk or the Permanent Secretary or CEO, ordinary folk or a national leader, can achieve success and satisfaction in different ways.

Don't Aim for Success

In Chapter 6 of *The Analects* (translated by James Legge), Confucius was asked about perfect virtue. The Master said, "The man of virtue makes the difficulty to be overcome his first business, and success only a subsequent consideration; this may be called perfect virtue."

One of my favourite books is Viktor Frankl's *Man's Search for Meaning*. In the Preface to the book, he wrote: "Don't aim at success – the more you aim at it and make it a target, the more you are going to miss it. For success like happiness cannot be pursued; it must ensue." It is useful to remember and be reminded that success and happiness are "the unintended side-effect of one's dedication to a cause greater than oneself".

What then is the cause greater than oneself that one should dedicate to? It reminds me of the Dexter Gate at Harvard Yard. There are 25 gates in Harvard Yard. In 1889, Samuel Johnston gave the funds to build the first gate to open into the Yard, but members of other classes soon followed his example to build the entryways. Dexter Gate (class of 1890) erected in 1901 is widely known for the inscription on its crest. Carved on the outside of the gate: "Enter to grow in wisdom." On the reverse side, as you leave Harvard Yard, another inscription reads "Depart to serve better thy country and thy kind." Dexter was president of his class at Harvard. He was expected to be a leader in the world. Tragically, his story ended just four years after his graduation, in 1894, when he died from cerebral spinal meningitis.

Let us grow in wisdom. Whichever career we choose, let us also dedicate our talents and wisdom to public service.

In both career and relationship, we give our best, but do not be expectant, do not feel entitled.

Stages of Life

Every one of us is different, and we may be at different stages in life. What we can contribute varies. Hindu philosophy traditionally observes four stages of life. These stages are known as *ashramas*. *Brahmacharya* is the first stage of life. It is the student stage of life, preparing for success in later stages of life. The second stage is called *Grihastha*. Known as the "householder" stage, it follows what most people do naturally after leaving school. *Vanaprastha* is the third stage. It begins after individuals fulfil their obligations to their families, choosing to spend more time giving back to their communities as they deepen their spiritual practice. The goal is to devote oneself to spiritual practice with a commitment to *seva* (selfless service) and in pursuit of *moksha* (liberation). The fourth stage is *Sannyasa,* renunciation. Having fulfilled all prior obligations, a person is free to devote himself entirely to spiritual growth. The goal is to attain liberation from the cycle of birth and rebirth.

If you are young, you are probably at the first two stages of life, busy preparing for success in later stages of life or busy at work.

In our younger days, we work hard building for success in career and family, striving to be the best we can be. We broaden our horizon, open to possibilities and imagination, learn new skills, focus, practise and gain expertise. Work well with others and get the best of our team, manage our bosses and our subordinates, make friends and build networks, invest in ourselves. Choose meaningful work, find meaning in our work and work meaningfully. We need to find the good in what we do, and do good. In the second half of our life, we find more time to give back to communities. This is also the time to live in the present and enjoy life, and treasure family and friends.

Many of my friends are in our 60s and 70s. We are at the third stage of life. We have largely fulfilled our obligations to our families and are now spending more time devoting to ourselves, and to serving others with our wisdom and sharing the things we believe are most important.

Staying Alive

When I went to Harvard Kennedy School of Government in 1987 for my mid-career MPA, I took the course "Conflict, Cooperation and Strategy" under Professor Thomas Schelling. Being from the military, the subject appealed to me. Schelling was a popular professor, not least because the talk in the school was that if any HKS professor were to win a Nobel Prize, it would be him. But when John Nash (*A Beautiful Mind*) won the Nobel Prize in Economics in 1994 for his game theory work, many people thought Schelling would not get it. I was happy to meet Schelling in August 1996 when he visited Singapore as a Lee Kuan Yew Distinguished Visitor. The objective of the programme is to invite internationally eminent and outstanding academics and scholars to Singapore to make high level contributions to National University of Singapore, Nanyang Technological University and Singapore in general. Then in 2005, at the age of 84, Schelling was awarded the Nobel Prize in Economics for "having enhanced our understanding of conflict and cooperation through game-theory analysis". As the Nobel Prize cannot be awarded posthumously, Schelling would not have achieved Nobel Prize success had he not remained fit and alive. Schelling went on to live to the age of 95.

Staying healthy and living a long life is important. Schelling might not have won the Nobel Prize had he not lived past 84. Amos Tversky, who had collaborated extensively with Daniel Kahneman and together published the work that would eventually win Kahneman the Nobel Prize in Economics in 2002, did not because he died in 1996 at age 59. Kahneman lived till 2024, aged 90.

Tversky's achievements were no less exceptional because he didn't win the prize. Martin Rees (Astronomer Royal, a former president of the Royal Society and past Master of Trinity College, Cambridge) wrote in an opinion piece published in *The Guardian* (12 October 2023) titled "Some Nobel winners are great intellects, others are lucky. There's more to science than these prizes". He suggested, "We need more and better ways of encouraging discovery and innovation. One possible route is 'challenge prizes', which don't reward past success but incentivise future efforts to tackle an important problem." Perhaps the point is that success should not be measured by a prize, even the Nobel Prize.

CHAPTER 16

Happiness

Four Levels of Happiness

Aristotle noted that happiness is the one thing you can choose for itself – everything else is chosen for the sake of happiness. Aristotle distinguished between four levels of happiness.

Happiness Level One: Laetus. Sensual gratification based on something external to the self – simple pleasure seeking. It is short-lived satisfaction and not what human happiness is all about.

Happiness Level Two: Felix. Ego gratification – the happiness of winning. "I have more of this than X." "I am better at this than X." This kind of happiness results from competition with another person. The self is seen in terms of how we measure up to others. We experience Felix when we get a promotion or a praise. However, such happiness is rather unstable and, if one fails, can lead to unhappiness and sense of worthlessness.

Happiness Level Three: Beatitudo (Beatitudo = happiness or blessedness). The happiness that comes from seeing the good in others and doing the good for others. It is, in essence, other-regarding action.

Happiness Level Four: Sublime beatitudo (sublime = to lift up or elevate). This encompasses a reach for fullness and perfection of happiness. The fullness, therefore, of goodness, beauty, truth and love.

Psychologists have labelled this desire for ultimate happiness a call for connection to a larger universe or a sort of transcendence. There is no definitive or universal answer to how to achieve this – spirituality and religion, public service, philosophy, art, scientific endeavours? You have to find your own calling.

Aristotle believed that the purpose and ultimate goal in life is to achieve eudaimonia ("happiness"). He believed that eudaimonia was not simply virtue, nor pleasure, but rather it was the exercise of virtue.

A key component of Aristotle's theory of happiness is the factor of virtue. He contended that in aiming for happiness, the most important factor is to have "complete virtue" or – in other words – good moral character.

Aristotle identified friendship as being one of the most important virtues in achieving the goal of eudaimonia. In fact, he valued friendship very highly, and described a "virtuous" friendship as the most enjoyable, combining both pleasure and virtue.

Aristotle went on to put forward his belief that happiness involves, through the course of an entire life, choosing the "greater good", not necessarily that which brings immediate, short-term pleasure.

Thus, according to Aristotle, happiness can only be achieved at the life-end: It is a goal, not a temporary state of being.

Eudaimonia is a lifelong goal.

The Harvard Study of Adult Development

The longest study ever conducted on human happiness – the Harvard Study of Adult Development – started more than 85 years ago in 1938 when scientists began tracking the health of 268 Harvard sophomores, hoping the longitudinal study would reveal clues to leading healthy and happy lives. The study eventually expanded the research to include the men's offspring as well as Boston inner-city residents.

Over the years, researchers have studied the participants' health trajectories and their broader lives, including their triumphs and failures in careers and marriage. The findings have shown that close relationships, more than money or fame, are what keep people happy throughout their lives. Those ties protect people from life's discontents, help to delay mental and physical decline, and are better predictors of long and happy lives than social class, IQ or even genes. That finding proved true across the board among both the Harvard men and the inner-city participants.

Robert Waldinger met with James Shaheen, editor-in-chief of *Tricycle: The Buddhist Review*, to discuss what makes a good life, the common regrets and how his Zen practice informs his work as a psychiatrist. The interview was published in *Tricycle Talks* "It's Never Too Late to Be Happy" Episode #83 with Robert Waldinger, 25 January 2023.

Shaheen put several questions to Waldigner such as what were some of the common regrets that people had towards the end of their lives. Elderly respondents felt they had spent too much time at work and less time with their loved ones. Other issues included the realisation that good relationships contribute to one's general well-being; relationships need to be nurtured, whether in the family, at work or socially.

It is a long interview but worth a read. I shall reproduce just two of Waldinger's sharing excerpted from that interview:

- *(On amount of time spent and how we spend our time.)* "Well, first, there's the amount of time spent. There was a fashionable school of thought for a while that said that it doesn't really matter how much time you spend with your developing child, it's really just the quality of the time. When you're there, be very present. And we know that's not true, that face time really matters, the amount of time matters. One of the things we know is that we can lose perfectly wonderful relationships by not spending enough time. I used to think my friends would always be my friends, and yet perfectly wonderful relationships can die away if we never call, if we never make time to see each other. The amount of time matters. What that does for me is it makes me be much more intentional about reaching out to people in my life whom I want to see regularly. So it's not just paying full attention when I'm there. It's making it happen in the first place. And then there's the other side of it, which is when I'm there, are we going to go to a coffee shop, have coffee together and spend the whole time on our phones, or are we really going to put our phones away, put our screens completely away, and just be there with each other. That's a different quality of interaction."

- *(On asking of our experience, "What's here that I've never noticed before?" and how that question can guide our interpersonal relationships?)* "I'll tell you about a research study that's relevant. They studied couples, and they studied how tuned in people were to their partner's feelings. They studied them early on in their relationship, like when they first started dating, and then 10, 15, 20 years into a relationship. And what they found was that couples who'd known each other 10, 15, 20 years were way less tuned in to their partner's feelings than they were when they were dating. When we're dating, we hang on this person's every look and word. Is this person into me? You get to a point where you feel like, 'Oh, I know everything about them.' My wife and I've been together 36 years, and I can lapse into that sense of

'Oh, I know her. I know how she's going to react.' That's the place to bring this beginner's mind. Suzuki Roshi has this famous quote, which I love. He said, 'In the beginner's mind, there are many possibilities. In the expert's mind, there are few.' So if I'm an expert on my wife, then I think I already know everything. If I can bring beginner's mind to having dinner tonight, then I can look and say: What's here that I haven't noticed before? What's she talking about? Or what's changed about her appearance or how she moves through the kitchen, whatever it might be, just to get myself to pay careful enough attention to find what's changed. As Buddhism tells us, and we know from our experience, everything is always changing. So what's here that I've never noticed before is actually asking us to pay attention to the process of continual change."

Leading Well, Living a Happy Life, a Life True to Myself

I try to live a happy life, a life true to myself, not the life others expect of me. Each of us has to develop our own leadership journey. In the process, we all learn and change. When I started my career, I was driven largely by Happiness Level One: Laetus and Happiness Level Two: Felix. Success was getting a promotion, winning a praise and achieving goals. As we get older, we begin to understand that promotion is not the holy grail of career success and happiness.

As managing gives way to a mix of leading and managing, we do not seek to solve problems too quickly but ask questions and try to define the correct problem to solve. We understand the importance of working as a team and in developing people. Our best people must be world-class and be able to compete with the best in the world. We treat all with respect and dignity, and gain the respect of others, including bosses whom we disagree with. We manage upwards, sideways and downwards. Happiness comes increasingly from Level Three and Four, from seeing the good in others, doing the good for others and serving society.

While public service work can be bureaucratic and the work hours long, serving people and the country is very meaningful. The work experience becomes so enjoyable that we love to do it for the sheer sake of doing it, that it has become, in Mihaly Csikszentmihalyi's words, a "flow". Of course, work in the private sector can be meaningful too. We need the private sector to grow the economy, to produce goods and services that people need and want. And if one were to work under a toxic leader in the public service, life can be very miserable and you may need a second career. The thing is, you must begin thinking about it long before you have to enter it. You must be able to see yourself say in 10-15 years' time. For some maybe when you are 50. For others, 55, 60, 65 even 70. What is your future life like? Is this what you hope you will become or might become?

And while we may experience flow in our work, we must remember that family and friends are important.

Importance of Family and Friends

I try to spend as much time with my family and friends as I can. We learn from one another as we share experiences, interests and perspectives. Good friends are good for our health. However, friends can grow apart due to differences in interests, views and values. Hence it is useful to heed the advice of Baltasar Gracian, the 17th century Jesuit scholar, that "Knowing how to keep a friend is more important than gaining a new one. Look for friends who can last, and when they are new, be satisfied that one day they will be old. The best ones of all are those well salted, and whom we have shared bushels of experience."

I try to meet up with university friends for brunch every third Wednesday of alternate months, often at a hawker centre, sometimes in a nice restaurant. I am a member of a diverse group that does nature and mindful walking at the Botanic Gardens and other nature parks on Saturday mornings, followed by breakfast. And I also meet up with secondary school friends, army mates, former civil service colleagues and social work volunteers. We can lose perfectly wonderful relationships by not spending enough time if we never call, if we never make time to see each other. We need to be much more intentional about reaching out to people in our life whom we want to see regularly.

How should one pursue happiness? It depends on what one understands happiness is.

Leadership

An Abridged Version of
J.Y. Pillay's Interview by Viswa Sadasivan in 2015[1]

I have never considered myself a great leader. However, I have been placed in positions where from time to time I had to exercise some leadership. To me, leadership means having integrity, to elicit trust, to delegate and to stimulate and draw ideas from the ground.

Outstanding bosses

I had two outstanding bosses: Hon Sui Sen and Goh Keng Swee. Both had a very strong sense of compassion which is important if you want to be a leader. There were also men of great competence: Lee Kuan Yew no doubt, Toh Chin Chye, S. Rajaratnam, and Lim Kim San.

Intrinsic attributes of a leader and his behavioural pattern

Hon Sui Sen and Goh Keng Swee had many qualities in common but their styles were different. We've got to maybe distinguish

---

[1]   Note: The original interview was conducted on 29 June 2015 over 84 minutes. It is an excellent interview, worth a careful read. The author and publisher have abridged the interview with Mr Pillay's permission for including in this book.

between the intrinsic attributes of a leader and his behavioural pattern. In terms of intrinsic qualities, I don't think there was that much difference between Dr Goh and Mr Hon. But their behavioural characteristics were certainly not identical. Both had a very strong sense of compassion, not just for the people reporting to them but for society at large. Very important factor if you want to be a leader. But when it came to the relationship between each of them and his subordinates, there were differences. Both were extremely loyal but Hon Sui Sen was a perfect gentleman. No matter what the circumstances may be, whether he woke up on the right side of the bed or not, it didn't matter at all. And you got the impression that every day he woke up on the right side of the bed.

On characteristics of leaders

We used to practise a form of job evaluation in the civil service. We considered three characteristics – first, the job knowledge, that is how much knowledge you need to do the job; second, what were the problem-solving demands of the job, and finally the accountability.

At the end of the day, you place leaders in two categories: action-oriented people is one category, thinkers is the other. Most leaders are in the second category of thinkers. Very reflective and deep thinking – those are the qualities you need in a leader.

Down the hierarchy are the action-oriented people: the foreman, the supervisor, the lower management – they have to deliver the goods. A leader can delegate authority but must be accountable for his subordinates' accountabilities.

On how to manage without micromanaging; without being too intrusive

That's why you got to have, if you're a good leader, a bit of horse sense up there. You have to be able to know what are the parameters that you will want to monitor closely. That does not mean you have to keep chasing your subordinates everyday. But you look at his reports. You also listen to his underlings without jeopardising his authority. That's a difficult task, to go two steps down. You don't want to do that too obtrusively, you've got to sort of welcome the feedback. And then somehow filter it and pass it on to the reporting officer below you.

On being decisive and yet listening

The worst thing is to shirk the responsibility of making a decision. Subordinates find that most annoying. Just make a decision; it doesn't matter if it is not the so-called correct decision. If there is a decision we'll all proceed. And if it doesn't lead anywhere, okay, you find some way, you're the leader, you find some way of rectifying it. Incidentally, I don't believe there is any such thing as a perfect decision. There are so many options. This option is perfect, everything else, no. Every option has pros and cons, and it's your job as the leader when it comes to the crunch to decide which you think is the best option. Your subordinates may not think that is the best option but they will follow you if you offer decisive leadership. And recognise you may not always be right.

On his "decision in the first couple of years as Chairman of SIA, in the early 70s, where he made the bold, calculated albeit, move to buy 19 Boeing aircraft, the famous 'sale of the century' accolade that was announced"

That particular decision wasn't made in the early years of the 1970s, it was towards the end of the 1970s, I can't remember when '77, '78? But we had an earlier decision, which was even more, I would say, controversial. Not controversial in the media in those days, but within upper reaches of the Government. It was the decision to buy the Boeing 747 aircraft. We made that decision in the board, it required a heck of a lot of money and we did need a government guarantee to the EXIM Bank of Washington D.C. I can't remember how many aircraft we placed an order for, whether it was four or seven. But it was a lot of money for us in those days, a small company. And Singapore didn't have the billions that it now has, managed by GIC, or the sovereign wealth funds. So the Cabinet got a bit queasy, and they quizzed us. Hon Sui Sen was the Finance Minister. They didn't summon me to the Cabinet to explain, thank goodness. We sent them a stack of documents that we used to do our evaluation and to make an assessment of our financial condition, the condition of our financial forecast. After that we never heard from the Cabinet. No veto, so we went ahead.

So that was the decision, which elicited a lot of concern by the Cabinet. But the second decision towards the end of the 1970s for, I don't know how many aircraft, 19, amounting to 900 million US dollars, which was the biggest at that time ever placed by any carrier so that's why we attracted world attention. That wasn't such a ground-breaking decision from our perspective.

The company, the board, or for that matter, the Cabinet. By that time the Cabinet was quite relaxed, it didn't put any query in our direction at all.

It was interesting how SIA developed in the 1970s. We were the only airline in Asia that had the gumption to do these, to think big. Nothing to do with me, I must confess, it all came from management. And we supported them. I could see it, I mean I must say, I had the responsibility of course. Supporting management when they brought these proposals to the board, not rejecting it. When I said no, it would have been no. But I had confidence in management, I knew them well. I saw their record and I noticed that all the carriers around us were so pusillanimous. Most of them were government-owned. No big ambitions, they just wanted a soft life.

On making the difference

What made us different? Well the Government told us, you guys you're on your own, no subsidy. And I think it would have been against our pride to accept any subsidy from the Government. We didn't want it. We say we could do our own thing and we defied the big powers, the IATA (International Air Transport Association), which laid down strict conditions about how much you can charge for a ticket and what you can serve on board and things like that. So all that needed a bit of iconoclasm. We were iconoclasts.

On the importance of focus

As a leader, you need to have focus, i.e., one principal objective. Don't be distracted. The focus may be the right decision or the wrong decision. A leader needs the ability to accept and acknowledge when the path taken is not working. If it's just not working, then you have no choice. In a sense it's forced upon you.

Just because you focus on an issue doesn't mean you wear blinkers. You're aware of what's going on around you, and if it's not going well, you begin to consider other options. What are those options? And it's also a question of how soon you react. Sometimes you just persist doggedly, and find that you've dug a deeper and deeper hole. Then you say stop, or maybe something has forced your hand, you have to stop.

On the need for a communitarian spirit

I think inside me I'm a socialist. And even outside. A socialist in the good sense. Not so much in the field of economics where I think socialists sometimes get funny ideas, controlling the levers of economic power, but on the social side. Always been like that since I was a little fellow.

Goh Keng Swee was exactly the same. He had some experience in the social services sector. He was actually from the Social Welfare Department. His PhD thesis, which incidentally, he completed in two years at LSE (the London School of Economics and Political Science), was based on of his experience in the Social Welfare Department, a statistical analysis. So, he too, I think had a very strong sense of, what do you call it, communitarian spirit. It's not a question of winner takes all; the winner has to share his good fortune.

On the need to be conscious of what's happening around you. And to study enough from the history of Singapore and what the founding fathers of modern Singapore, I mean PAP Government of the '50s and '60s, what their concentrations were.

Don't forget PAP (People's Action Party) was a socialist party, that's what Lee Kuan Yew said, we are an Asian, socialist, non-communist, democratic, those were the four main attributes. People forgot about the socialism after some time, maybe it was also partly the doing of the founding fathers of modern Singapore. They were doing a lot of things for the underdog, the housing programmes, HDB (Housing and Development Board) programme started right at the beginning of the '60s before even the Economic Development Board was set up. They recognised the importance of those things and then health, education, moved quite nicely.

On the need for greater awareness of the uncertainties before us

What I would like to see among leaders in Singapore is greater awareness of the uncertainties before us. To realise that there's no such thing as an absolutely right decision. They've got to be humble enough to recognise that, to be always conscious of other strands of opinion and other constituencies. I'm not suggesting that leadership in Singapore is deficient, not at all. In fact, I think they're trying very hard, leaders in every walk of life in Singapore are trying very hard to take this need into account without necessarily rationalising it. They do it; it comes, you may say subliminally. Not naturally but subliminally because they're conscious of what's going on around them, not just in Singapore but in the world.

Not being too arrogant, I think sometimes Singaporeans tend to be rather arrogant. I'm not pessimistic about the future of Singapore but I think we sometimes have to inject a little more humility.

ABOUT J.Y. PILLAY

Mr J.Y. Pillay was Chairman of the Presidential Council of Advisors from 2005 to 2019. He was one of Singapore's top ranking civil servants, having been the Permanent Secretary in many key ministries, including finance, defence and national development. He was the first Chairman of Singapore Airlines from 1972 to 1996. He retired from the civil service in 1995.

Index

www.ingramcontent.com/pod-product-compliance
Lightning Source LLC
Chambersburg PA
CBHW051954270326

41929CB00015B/2646